KNIFECRAFT

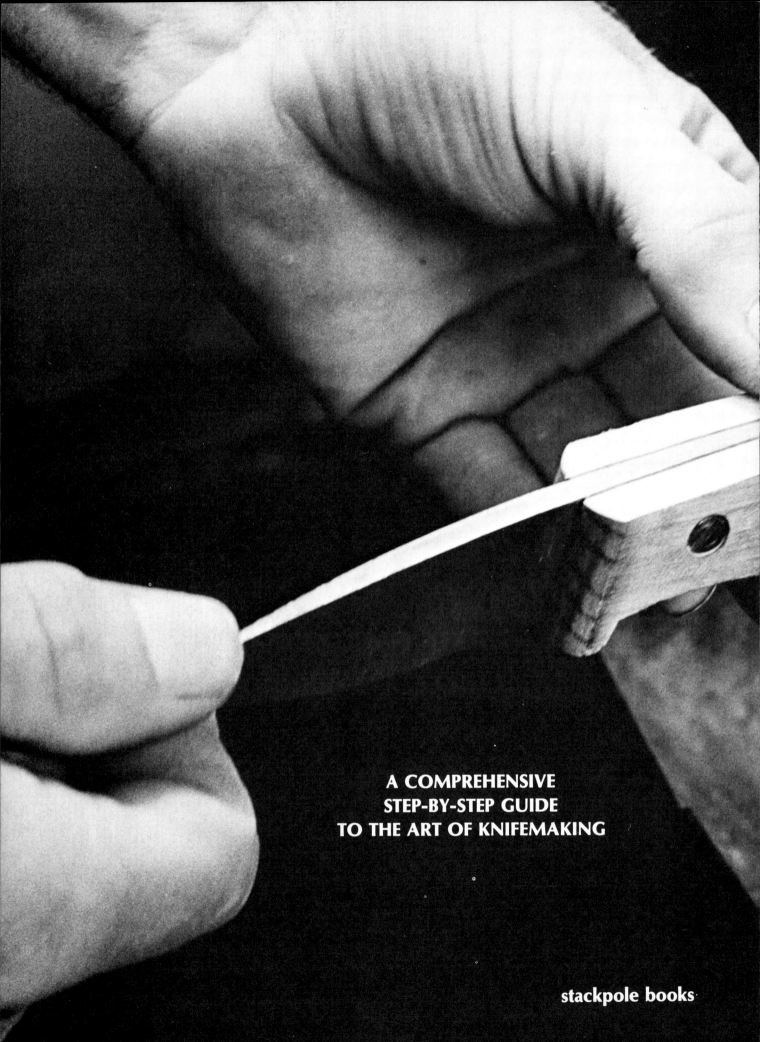

A COMPREHENSIVE
STEP-BY-STEP GUIDE
TO THE ART OF KNIFEMAKING

stackpole books

KNIFECRAFT

Sid Latham

Knifecraft

Copyright © 1978 by Sid Latham

Published by
STACKPOLE BOOKS
Cameron and Kelker Streets
P.O. Box 1831
Harrisburg, Pa. 17105

Published simultaneously in Don Mills, Ontario, Canada by
Thomas Nelson & Sons, Ltd.

LIBRARY OF CONGRESS CATALOGING IN PUBLICATION DATA
Latham, Sidney
    Knifecraft
    Includes index.
    1. Knives. I. Title.
TS380.L29 1978   621.9′3   78–16825
ISBN 0-8117-0927-2

Printed in the United States of America

To my mother
with thanks for everything

CONTENTS

PREFACE

The artistry of the craftsmen shown in these pages is, in many instances, truly awesome. Knifemaking has been called an art form, and indeed, that is true. These knifemakers are artists in wood and metal, shaping and forming a utilitarian tool into something of grace and beauty.

Handcrafting a knife is not entirely new; it has been done throughout the centuries in many lands. The rise of the modern handmade knife in our country, however, only began in the early 1930s, and the ensuing forty-odd years have seen it brought to a degree of perfection that has, at times, amazed even the craftsmen themselves.

Much of the high-quality workmanship shown is due, in part, to the members of the Knifemakers Guild, who vie with each other, in unspoken competition, at their yearly guild show and meeting. One year it was Ron Lake with his unusual folders who made a lasting impression on both his colleagues and the buying public. It took just that long for Lake to become a legend in his own time. The first show that Corbet Sigman attended shot him upward to that league of makers known as Master Craftsmen, who do everything with impeccable taste and skill. Later it was Billy Mace Imel's turn to impress his peers, and finally a fellow named Buster Warenski came out of the West and his knives said it all.

As the years went on, new men joined the guild with work equal to or even surpassing many famous names. This is as it should be because these craftsmen come together not only to exchange views and techniques but also to gain inspiration for the future.

In the beginning the working knife or sportsman's blade that could be used in the field was in the forefront of most makers' offerings. Then the collectibles, or art knives, came along, with magnificently etched blades, ivory handles, and perhaps, sheaths tipped with gold or silver. Hence collectors began, in a subtle manner, to patronize makers of their choice, and the results made a valuable contribution to knifemaking because these knives pushed the knife craftsman to the limits of skill and design. The line between a practical working knife and one crafted for decor alone is thin, indeed. There is nothing wrong in having a pretty field knife hanging from a belt, and if given proper care, it will last as well and as long as other outdoor gear.

In crafting knives most of these men, at one time or another, began as tinkerers, hobbyists, or outdoorsmen who were unhappy with the cutting steel available. But no matter how magnificent today's offerings, that first blank of steel had to be ground out, fitted with a handle, and used in the field. Rare is the man who can shape something perfect the first time the effort is made. Trial and error is the norm rather than perfection, and I am certain that many of the master cutlers in this book would hesitate to show their very first effort.

Since this is a book about knifemaking as well as knifemakers, we shall also be discussing the wide choice of steels available and the many designs and types of knives that can be created. A knife is no longer a simple tool with a sharp edge and a handle to guide it, but is something rather more complex than once imagined.

The beginning knifemaker must have among his virtues the important one of patience. He need not be concerned with integrity, because he has no one to please except himself and the skills required to make a knife may be improved upon with time. But a lack of patience means the trash bin will be filled more quickly with scraps of steel and blocks of wasted wood. Any knifemaker of merit will advise the beginner to move slowly and gain the skills necessary to make a knife. There is no magic or mystery—just patience.

Acknowledgments

Over the past ten years knifemaking has grown in size from a handful of men crafting blades for the sportsman to a collector's market of knives ornate in design with fancy sheaths, etching, and rare and expensive materials for the handle.

Prices have grown, too, and a knife from a master cutler that sold for $75 a half-dozen years ago has climbed to well over $100 today. However, new men entering the field have realized that modest prices will help them sell knives and eventually gain acceptance with their peers and the public.

Most of these fine craftsmen have become friends over the years. I have stayed in their homes and spent many hours in their shops discussing many things. They have imparted knowledge and been free with advice and suggestions in all my writings about the field they love.

To the knifemakers who toiled for specific chapters in this book go my thanks—in particular, to George Herron and Jack Barnett, Bill Moran and Howard Viele, and that master of the decorated blade, Lloyd Hale. All these men invited me into their workshops and made special knives for this book. My thanks also go to Sherrill Shaw and Leonard Leibowitz, whose artful etchings have graced the blades of many craftsmen.

To the many knifemakers who lent me knives for photography and those collectors, in particular Ted Devlet and William P. Semon, Jr., who loaned me valuable knives from their collections also goes my appreciation for their kindness.

A special note of thanks to Andy Russell, who never fails to make invaluable suggestions and gives aid whenever asked. And, finally, to all those members of the Knifemakers Guild who have helped in many ways over the years also go my thanks and appreciation.

1

KNIVES AND THEIR MAKERS: A BRIEF BACKGROUND

During the late 1960s handmade knives began to grow in popularity, and what started as a craze for custom cutlery at that time shows no signs of diminishing. It is an accepted fact that the benchmade knife is here to stay, and with the growing number of craftsmen joining the ranks almost weekly there should soon be enough knives in our country to outfit every sportsman and his entire family properly for many years to come.

While the handcrafted knife isn't new, old-timers Bill Scagel and Harry Morseth have long since gone to the great grinding wheel in the sky; but along with John Cooper, Rudy Ruana, and Bo Randall, they started the acceptance of well-made cutlery for the sportsman. Of course, steels as well as skills have improved to the point where it can safely be said that today's outdoorsmen have offered to them for their approval the finest knives in history.

Certainly, with a great tradition of fine handiwork in our past, there still seems to be a yearning in modern man for something handmade, something that is almost near perfection that was crafted with pride. Those sportsmen demanding enough, and willing to pay the price, began to seek out knife specialists in little towns and villages with strange-sounding names like Pahokee, Whitefish, Mesa, Pioneer. In fact, sometimes even their neighbors did not know that these men were knifemakers. Knifemakers? My God, imagine walking into a bank and telling the loan officer you make knives for a living. Well, that did happen a couple of times, but with books and magazines spreading the gospel, the craftsmen slowly began to gain the respect they so richly deserve.

Perhaps the one man most directly responsible for the fad in fine cutlery is Bo Randall, Jr. It is history now, of course, how Randall found an old Scagel knife being used to scrape the bottom of a boat and decided to emulate the old Michigan craftsman. Now, more than thirty years later, Randall has a small knife factory in Orlando, Florida, with more than a dozen craftsmen turning out hand-forged knives in the traditional manner. Randall, the acknowledged dean of American knifemakers, not only had the skills to design fine knives but also the ability to publicize custom-crafted knives and have them accepted by the buying public. Bob Loveless once said: "It's Randall's fault the rest of us are in the knife business." The fact that Randall knives have been carried by more fighting men, sportsmen, and expeditions than all other knives combined has played no small part in the growing interest in benchmade knives.

But if Randall laid the groundwork, others were swift to follow. Bob Loveless soon found his popularity growing, and no serious sportsman would even consider going afield without a Loveless drop-point hitched to his belt. Ted Dowell, a college professor when he began grinding blades, became so busy he had to become a full-time knifemaker to supply his customers. Others, now considered old-timers, had been making knives for a number of years. Dan Dennehy, Chubby Hueske, Clyde Fischer, Ralph Bone, Bill Moran, and a few more had done the groundwork in testing practical designs, experimenting with steels, and in general, had paid their dues. A half-dozen years ago there were only thirty or so men grinding steel; now, by actual count, there are nearly three hundred knifemakers, and those are only the men we know about. The list grows longer each day.

What is there about a handmade knife that grabs the imagination of most men? In truth, many are simply fascinated by gleaming steel, while others demand something unusual and unique. But it is difficult to give any one answer. The skill of a particular maker, certainly, but something different, something better, something crafted of the ultimate steel with a handle of rare exotica from the far corners of the earth, and finally, something that is one-of-a-kind. All of these combine to make a knife that many men willingly pay a few weeks', or even a few months', salary for. A knife that may be carried on the hunt of a lifetime, or perhaps just kept in a den to be admired and never used. There is a mystique about knives that is almost impossible to explain.

Where modern knifemaking began is almost as difficult to pin down. Some say the rash of articles in the sporting press saw the dawn of fine custom cutlery in our country. As the popularity of many fine craftsmen slowly emerged beyond their own small boundaries, observant sportsmen saw these marvelous knives and demanded one for themselves. No doubt, too, the continued success of Randall created a vacuum that pulled in every man who ever ground steel. Call them what you want—handmade, benchmade, or custom-crafted—these knives started a craze that shows no sign of abating.

In the early days of modern knifemaking, meaning only ten or twelve years ago, there were some pretty solid talents about, and equally, a few knifemakers who did not deserve to sell their wares at any price. As with any field where there is the gleam of gold, the charlatans soon appeared who took deposits, made promises, and swiftly disappeared into the nearby hills. Even today there are those who do not answer mail, accept telephone calls, or attempt to keep promised delivery dates. Fortunately, many of these gentlemen are no longer around, and knifemaking is slowly beginning to stand on its own merits.

But back to knives for a moment. The serious question of why all the fuss about a handcrafted knife is well taken. After all, good knives can be purchased

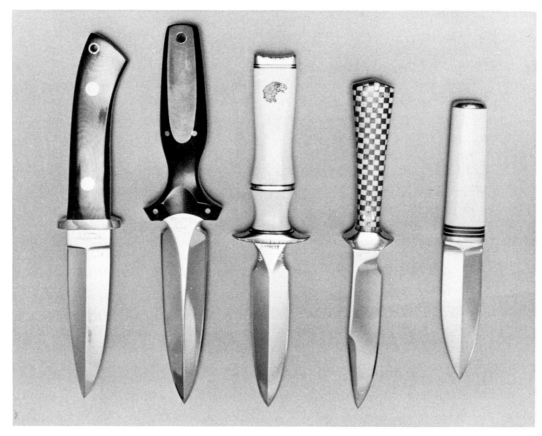

Boot knives by (left to right) Frank Centofante, Rod Chappel, Jack Barnett, Dragon Knives; and a Morseth sleeve knife.

in most hardward or sporting goods stores. It's more than that. Ten years ago there were few commercial cutlery firms who could turn out a practical, sensible knife of quality workmanship, good design, or even the right steel. The average hunting knife was a fairly long contraption, concocted of cheap alloys, that could be purchased for about $10 or less. When the first benchmade knife came along for about $35 it was a real bargain, and it made some of the more progressive cutlery firms take notice. Now all that has changed. The factory product has been gradually upgraded since the surge of benchmade knives, and well-designed factory blades are now being produced from good steels. The average sportsman can now purchase a good commercially produced knife for less than a custom job cost a few years ago, and if he really wants to blow a lot of money, he can still get a handmade knife for about $60.

The men of the Knifemakers Guild had a lot to do with this. In the beginning, like all fledgling organizations, there were some growing pains. One president resigned, the secretary quit, and out of this turmoil grew greater problems. In the end it all wound down, and the group is now a fairly happy family of strong-willed individualists who seem reasonably sociable at their annual shindig. Bear in mind that many of these men, and a few women, live in fairly remote and inaccessible areas of the country, and the terrain and climate may have made more of a mark on their personalities than they themselves realize. This is not to imply that knifemakers are difficult to get along with. In fact, the opposite is true, although a few, admittedly, are seemingly impossible. Like all creative human beings, knifemakers have their moments of greatness, and as long as this greatness shows through when turning out a knife, that's all anyone can or should ask for. What many people forget is that when one is dealing with a knifemaker, one is dealing with a true artist. Although the maker isn't a god, he is a craftsman in wood and steel, and in a few cases, a creative genius in his assembly of all those bits and pieces of steel and wood and the skill that finally makes a magnificent knife—a knife that is good to look at, that cuts better than most knives previously owned, and that carries in it something of the artist-craftsman.

Sportsmen obviously liked what they saw and orders began to pile up. Master craftsmen like Corbet Sigman, Bill Moran, Jess Horn, Bob Loveless, Ted Dowell, and a handful of others became so busy that orders could not be filled for 18 months. That was in the beginning, and now it is said that Loveless won't take any orders for at least five years, and Bill Moran, the master of the Damascus blade, must ask his customers to wait perhaps ten years. It's easy to see that with such popularity, a knife collector may not even get a desired knife in his lifetime.

Is it like this with every knifemaker? No, it is not. And such quality craftsmen as Jim Small, Harold Corby, Mike Franklin, Fred Carter, Dwight Towell, or Sid Birt will get a first-class knife to their customers within a year. What caused the long waiting lines for particular makers isn't obvious to many observers, but when Lloyd Hale began his fancy file work on knives, almost every craftsman thought: "Gosh, if Hale can get $800 or more for a knife, I'll do the same." Well, it didn't turn out that way. The collectors that Hale was creating his museum pieces for were discerning buyers, and only a handful of steel grinders made the grade. While creative craftsmen swell the ranks of knifemaking, only a very small group have reached the top of their craft and become household words.

Buster Warenski is one such artisan whose work is in great demand for its perfection of execution. Rod Chappel is another superb knifemaker popular with collectors and Jess Horn makes exquisitely finished folders and some small boot knives that aficionados clamor for. It is said that Horn sold out his entire display at the 1976 Knifemakers show within 15 minutes and had to go home in an armored car. The rest of the time he sat there writing orders, and most avid collectors will have to wait a couple of years for those orders to be filled.

The arrival of collectors on the scene has not been without problems. Name makers must keep their customers waiting, and almost every knifemaker wants to sell to collectors, many charging outrageous prices their talents don't deserve. On the other hand, for example, many fine craftsmen didn't sell a single knife at the 1976 Guild show. Even those who were making practical knives priced well under $100 packed their wares at the end of the three-day run and went home sadder, but one wonders if any wiser.

Bill Moran has frequently stated that we are living in the Golden Age of Knifemaking. That may be true for those with the stature of a Moran, but for others trying to eke out a living grinding steel, the gold may have tarnished a little. Fortunately, many without talent have dropped out, and others will have to be discovered beyond their own small towns. Many new craftsmen deserve special attention. J. D. Clay, a highly skilled knifemaker still in his twenties, does magnificent work and sells a beautifully made knife for about $75. Rade Hawkins, another new name in the field, does excellent work and offers a selection of popular steels and knives with finely tapered tangs. Sid Birt, a weaponry instructor with the air force, recently showed his wares, and they can stand alongside any maker's knives. Birt is also a specialist in combat knives and offers a wide variety of boot and fighting knives. From the high country of Alaska come Dan and Ron Isaacs, a father-and-son team, who craft practical and sensible (meaning about 3-inch blades) knives at affordable prices. Virgil England is another Alaskan, who spends time roaming the high country when he isn't grinding blades, and A. W. Amoureux, who lives in Anchorage, also makes excellent woodsman's knives.

Not all of today's craftsmen began as full-time knifemakers. Ron Lake, who caused a furor with his fine, uniquely designed folders a few years ago, was a tool and die maker who, because of his perfection in constructing fine folders, is now a full-time maker and is usually behind in orders. Horace Wiggins owns a couple of department stores in Louisiana and Texas and obviously does not have to grind steel for a living, yet he crafts some of the most unusual knives extant. Wiggins's forte is odd and unusual materials for his knife handles. Such exotica as sea shells embedded in clear epoxy and chula cactus or abalone shell are only a few of the interesting materials used. Incidentally, Wiggins works in one of the finest knife shops in the country.

Bernard "Bernie" Sparks is a schoolteacher in Idaho and is a much-under-rated knifemaker who turns out a first-class product. He is also one of the early makers, and each time his work is viewed, it shows improvement. Dan Dennehy, another solid craftsman, lives in Del Norte, Colorado. Dennehy gained fame during the Vietnam conflict with combat and survival knives. Although he still crafts an unusual stiletto, which is popular with undercover law enforcement agents, he has turned more and more to the sportsman who wants a neat, usable knife for the field. D'Alton Holder of Phoenix, Arizona, works for the local power company and makes superb knives for both the collector and knife user. All these men turn out well-crafted knives at honest prices, although the term "honest" may mean different things to different people. Obviously, a good knife with Micarta handles should sell for under $100, and sometimes for that price the lucky buyer may be offered a choice of tropical woods or even Sambar stag. Naturally, such exotica as ivory, amber, jade, or other rarities are going to raise the price, and the buyer should expect to pay more for such knives—if not willingly, he should at least realize what he is getting. Fancy file work around the butt cap, on the guard, or along the spine of the blade will soon bring the knife into the collector's realm, and combined with a well-carved ivory handle, with perhaps an inlay or wrapping of gold or silver wire, will command such an astronomical price that all but the wisest collector will blanch. What the knowledgeable knifeman knows is that such an "art" knife from a top-name maker is also a solid investment. Those who purchased knives such as these only a few years ago could realize enormous profits if they were to sell them today.

A handsomely engraved folder from an artist like Henry Frank, obtained at full price three or four years ago, could easily double, and in some cases triple, in value. Another folder from Ron Lake purchased for perhaps $100 a half-dozen years ago would now bring, at the very least, $500. These two are folders, but what of the straight-blade knife? Sheath knives from some of the quality craftsmen have also moved upward in value.

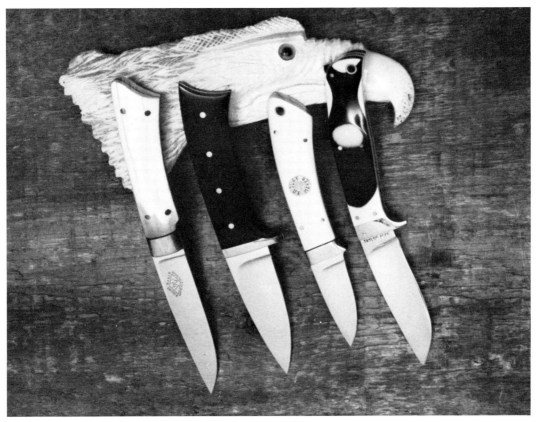

Small, modern blade styles with various handle materials. (Left to right) A knife by Horace Wiggins with a fossil ivory handle; a medium hunter by Charles Weiss; a small sportsman's model by J. D. Clay with an ivory Micarta handle; and a multicolored Micarta knife by Taylor Agee.

Ted Dowell's knives provide a good example. A few years back when Ted came up with the idea of an integral-hilt knife, the obvious successor was both an integral hilt and a butt. Since this knife is crafted from a block of steel weighing more than a couple of pounds and involves a lot of precise work on the milling machine, Ted had to charge $250 for this ultimate example of the knifemaker's art. Customers waited in long lines for many years to obtain one of these beauties. With the price of steel climbing upward, as with everything else in this world, Ted had to raise his price to $375. Those who already own these knives could double their price if they wanted to sell since the keen collector just does not want to wait a couple of years to add something new to his collection.

Bill Moran, of whom more later, is another example of a fine maker whose knives are a good investment. Moran has spent many years learning the secrets of crafting and forging Damascus blades. When they were first introduced they were priced at *$100 per inch of blade.* The price slowly crept to $125 and now stands at $200 per inch. No one knows, least of all Bill Moran, how long these prices will hold. If you then add extra charges for fancy additions like ivory or ebony handles, it can easily be seen that these handsome blades aren't for the man who wants to carve a turkey for Thanksgiving dinner.

Added to the enthusiasm for knives are the many knife shops that have

A wide range of folders. (Top to bottom) A beautifully engraved Henry Frank knife with silver bolsters and a moose horn handle; a Bob Ogg model with a mesquite handle; special Gerber presentation with covers of Oregon ice agate and engraved bolsters by Robert Valade of Cove, Oregon; a lightweight Morseth folder designed by A. G. Russell; an ornate folder with intricate file work by Harvey McBurnette; a Frank Centofante model; a small ivory-handled Ogg model; and a small folder designed by the author with a polished bone handle.

come into being since the phenomenon of handmade knives. There is Knife World in Englewood, Colorado; The Knife Shop, run by knifemaker Don Couchman at El Paso's International Airport; Gillie & Co., in Cos Cob, Connecticut; The Ramrod Knife & Gun Shop in New Castle, Indiana; and the Acorn Shop, which bills itself as "The World's Largest Knife Shop," in Gatlinburg, Tennessee. Most of these stores offer a wide selection of fine custom cutlery alongside the wares of such top commercial outfits as Gerber, Schrade, Western, and Case.

Of course, many knife buyers may resent the premium paid for purchasing a custom knife from a shop. "After all, why should I pay more than the maker's price?" It's an oft-asked question and the answer, frankly, is that the shopowner began standing in line a couple of years ago, laid down his cash, and wants an honest return on his investment. Besides, he usually offers a wide selection of fine knives from name makers, which gives the potential buyer the privilege of walking out with the knife of his choice.

But enough of collectors and fancy knives. What of the man who just wants a practical knife for everyday use? Where should he go and what should he require in a knife? One added advantage of the knife boom is that it has made knife users better informed. Articles and books have kept the knife-happy public abreast of trends. Added to that, modern designs of most knives have, at long last, done away with monster blades and heavy hunks of steel that caused the sportsman to walk leeward.

Bob Loveless, probably more than any craftsman, has influenced modern knife design with his dropped-point blade. A trim, sleek-looking knife, the blade design allows the user to quarter and section game with less danger to the animal's innards and thus avoid spoiling meat. Short blades are now the norm, and anything from 3 to 4 inches is considered practical in the field. The handle can be the buyer's choice, but Micarta is probably the least expensive material for a working knife. It is the standard handle offered by most knifemakers. Fancy woods are good; stag is traditional; but leave the rare and unusual to the collector. Remember, too, in spite of all that has been written and said to elevate the knife to the status of a museum piece, it is still a basic tool for sportsmen in the field. It should be used for cutting meat, for which it was originally intended, perhaps preparing food in camp, but really for nothing else. Go the pry-bar route, open cans, or use it for throwing, and forget it. All it will accomplish is to ruin the knife and invalidate the maker's guarantee. And speaking of guarantees, most honest craftsmen give the buyer the right to try a knife for a reasonable amount of time, and if he's displeased or unhappy for any reason, he may return it for a full refund. Obviously, if there is any deliberate harm, all bets are off. As Bob Loveless says, "We both know enough about knives and steels to know when a knife has been abused. If that happens, you'll find me asking some pretty hard questions."

Where to buy the knife brings up some problems. Send $1 or more to most knifemakers and you'll receive a catalog of goodies and lots of promises that should, on occasion, be taken with a grain of salt. The quality of most knives will be excellent, but getting the knife is, let us say, frequently difficult. This is not to impugn the honesty of knifemakers, and a complaint to the Knifemakers Guild will usually result in some action. But many of those making and selling knives for a living are bad businessmen, and, in a few instances, are downright dishonest. As

Two fine sheath knives by Dan Dennehy. The white handle is of ivory and the darker handle is of Micarta.

to deposits, that is something that any buyer will have to decide for himself. A word of advice would be not to send too much money—and then hope for the best. Many of the biggest names in knifemaking have been guilty of laxity in the treatment of customers. If that happens to you, go to the next knifemaker and try again.

The best education for anyone new to the world of knives is to visit a knife show and talk to the maker. Personal contact is important, and if it's a big show, there will be more knives for sale than anyone could afford in a lifetime.

No one can become a knife expert overnight; yet visits to a knife show, talking to both the knifemakers and collectors, and reading books and magazine articles will enhance anyone's knowledge of knives. When buying a knife there are areas of craftsmanship that should be examined with care. These include bevels, smooth fit of handle material, good grind, fine solder joints where the guard meets the blade, the straightness of the blade, and a fine polish. In general, does the knife look good and feel comfortable in the hand? Equally important to consider is whether the price is comfortable, too. Corbet Sigman or Buster Warenski, and a handful of others, have the right to command high prices for their products. The new man in town has to prove himself—not only to his peers, but to the knife-buying public as well.

Of late, many of the commercial cutlery firms have been shamed by the custom makers and forced to upgrade their steels and styles. A few years ago, Schrade Cutlery's Henry Baer assigned Bob Loveless the task of designing a knife of 154-CM steel that could be commercially produced. Schrade was delighted with the knife, and it was a success.

Gerber Legendary Blades is another quality company that stays atop the market with a continual flow of innovative designs and excellent steels. Stainless steel 440-C is used by Gerber in many models, and high-carbon tool steels are also used in the Gerber line. Al Mar, who heads up Gerber's design section, is both a brilliant designer and an experienced hunter who knows what will work on his many field trips. Western Cutlery in Boulder, Colorado, is slowly joining the more progressive cutlery outfits with a modern drop-point folder, produced by some advanced manufacturing techniques, that should sell well.

If custom knifemaking has done nothing else in the past ten years, it has forced the large knife outfits to look inward and find out what was wrong and take stock.

To get around some of these problems, a number of sportsmen have begun to make their own knives. Some for fun, others for more practical reasons, and a few because they like making knives the same way some men enjoy leather-work, building radio-controlled model planes, or constructing an entire railroad in the basement. Many of these aspiring craftsmen are fascinated by the skills of crafting their own knife and will soon try their hand at turning out a usable blade. The first effort may often be a disaster—some professional knifemen frankly admit they've made hundreds of blades before being completely satisfied with the results, while others have the rare ability to succeed with their first effort.

A few hobbyists, because they find blade-grinding too difficult or don't want to invest in expensive machinery, use kits and only construct the handle on a fully finished blade. There is a growing interest in this area, and a number of companies now offer complete kits as well as single blades in various stages of finish.

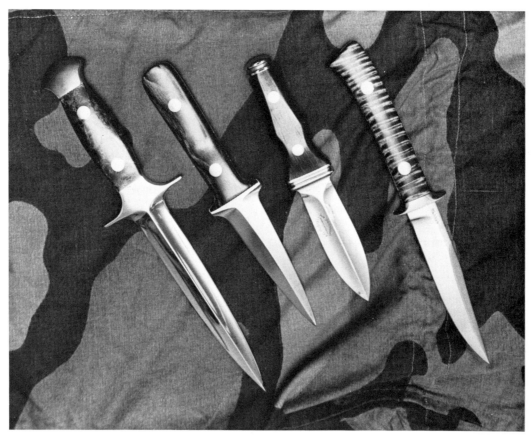

A range of blade styles on fighting and boot knives. (Left to right) A stiletto by Billy Mace Imel with a walnut burl handle; two rosewood daggers by Morseth; and a fine tiger tail maple-handled knife by master cutler George Herron.

Morseth Knives, under the direction of Andy Russell, is one company that will supply blades, spacers, guards, and Micarta for handles.

In 1976, Fred Smith of Fair Oaks, California, offered a custom folder for sale in kit form. Known as the Bildyur Knife Kit, it comes with a blade, springs, and back strap already heat-treated. Even the blade is preground. All the craftsman has to do is apply some finishing touches.

The fascination of crafting a knife is the pride of making something that can be used and, perhaps, allows a bit of bragging in the bargain. Most of these hobby knifemakers do not sell their knives; usually, they are given to friends, and the production is small enough that it does not interfere with the custom crafts-man.

Ron Eisen, an executive with the Stanley Works in New Britain, Connect-icut, had been assembling knives for a number of years. Ted Sittle, a retired bus-inessman in Denver, Colorado, goes the whole route, from designing the blades to grinding the steel. Ted has made a number of small, practical knives over the years and most are carried by friends.

A New York attorney, Joseph Mangiaracina, is both an avid knife collec-tor and a knifemaker. Joe feels that knifemaking is as good a hobby as any and prob-ably requires more skill than most. Paul Mobley is yet another amateur craftsman

An interesting selection of knives by amateur knifemen. The first two on the left are blades from Van Sickle Cutlery with handles by Bob Heidell; the third knife is a Morseth blade completed by Ron Eisen; and the small Micarta-handled knife was made by a retired Denver businessman, Ted Sittle.

who became fascinated with knives when he purchased a Randall a few years ago. A treasury agent from Provost, Utah, Mobley has made more than 35 knives from O-1 steel, ranging in size from skinners to big-bladed Bowies. In fact, Mobley has become so skilled he even does his own scrimshaw on ivory handles. Another New York lawyer, Bob Heidell, purchases his blades from Van Sickle Cutlery in Texas and puts on first-class handles. Frank Collura, an industrial designer, has made his own blades from 154-CM steel using nothing but files to form and shape the blade. Collura says, "This isn't something I'd recommend just anybody doing. It took so long that everytime I'd pass the piece of steel I'd pick up a file and give it another couple of swipes. The second knife I cut with a bandsaw because 154-CM is too difficult to cut by hand." Collura had both blades heat-treated commercially and then used paduk and bubinga for the handles. His sheaths were unusual in that both have brass mesh liners to allow the leather to breath and also to prevent the steel from touching the leather.

But this is only a small cross section of those making their own knives. For any man who wants to make a knife from start to finish, obviously some skills are required. He must know how to use hand tools in the beginning and slowly graduate to machines that will cut, drill, and grind if he plans to move on to the complete job of making a knife.

Two fine knives completely handmade without machines by New York industrial designer Francesco Collura. The sheaths are also designed and crafted by the maker and feature fine copper wire mesh lining to protect the steel from touching leather.

It might be fair at this point to define exactly what a handmade knife is. Is it a knife made completely by hand without any machines or equipment other than hand tools, or is it a knife where a minimum of grinders and buffers are used? There is one man, Bob Read of Nashville, who makes pocket knives with files and lots of muscle power. The only piece of electric equipment used is a small hand drill, set in a vise, for drilling the holes for pivot pins and rivets. Read's knives could certainly be called handmade in the truest sense of the word. On the other hand, today's cutlers who craft these expensive benchmade knives certainly use modern equipment. One reason is time, and the other is that these specialized high-speed machines will do a better job, be more exacting in control, and deliver a knife that will be as perfect as human skills can make it. Corbet Sigman is a master cutler who crafts a knife with perfection—collectors and his peers will concede that; yet Corbet feels that once a knife is placed in a jig, the knife is no longer handmade. "The knife must be held in the hands during all operations to justify its claim as a handmade knife," is the way Corbet feels about it.

We have just about reached that point where the reader must be wondering if he has the courage to make a knife. In search all these years for what is known as the perfect knife and still not happy, the thought naturally arises, "Should I make my own?" Sure, give it a try. It won't necessitate selling all your personal possessions, getting a divorce, or giving the kids to grandma. Knifemaking really

A Morseth kit with completed blade, soldered guard, and all other parts necessary to make a knife.

isn't a mystery at all—although some of those "good ole boys" at the knife shows may try to convince you it is. What it does take, however, is a fair amount of skill in the beginning and lots and lots of patience to emulate the craftsmen in this book.

Probably the simplest way of getting into knifemaking is to do as Ron Eisen or Bob Heidell have done, that is , order a couple of blades from one of the supply houses and try a hand at finishing the blades and putting on a handle. The blades of Indian Ridge Traders may satisfy the historical fan since their styles include both a Bowie and an Arkansas Toothpick. Morseth Knives offers a wide range of sportsmen's blades in various lengths, and they may be purchased with a nickle silver guard already soldered in place.

The aspiring knifemaker must take care in crafting a knife because sloppy workmanship will be very obvious. But once a few kits have been made, the next step is to make a blade with files and hand tools alone. Kits are not all that difficult, and bear in mind that it isn't necessary to have been the designer of the space shuttle or have the skills to do a corneal transplant to craft a knife. Apart from some small experience working with tools and some skills in working metal, the crafting of a practical hunting knife is within the capabilities of most home craftsmen. Up to this point the biggest problem was forming a worn-out file, industrial hacksaw blade, or a car spring into a blade. Although the result may be worth a

After epoxy is applied, the screw is tightly taken up and the knife is allowed to set overnight.

Finer and finer grades of paper are used to reduce the handle to its final shape.

The completed knife. Kits such as these are best for the novice maker and will introduce you to the skills necessary for knifemaking.

prize at a knife show, the practical value of the blade may be worthless, because of the steel. Now with kits available for almost any type of knife desired, the tough part of knifemaking, grinding the blade, has been eliminated.

By all means begin with a kit. It will deliver a better knife, at least for the beginning knife craftsman, and introduce the skills required to undertake the more demanding work that comes later. Remember, the most important ingredient is patience; the second is care.

2

WHAT IS A KNIFE?

The experienced knifeman may want to skip the next few pages while we discuss the parts of a knife for the benefit of the novice. Although knife nomenclature has been discussed in other tomes, a review will be useful here.

A knife, any knife, has a number of parts that if understood make the entire business of knives and knifemaking a bit easier to grasp. To the lay person a knife has two parts: a blade and a handle. Little thought is given to what is underneath the handle, how it is fastened, or what the various parts of a blade are for. To start at the beginning, blades come in a variety of sizes, shapes, and forms. There are even some odd-looking types like the Eskimo Ooloo, crafted by Dan Dennehy or Frank Hendricks. Blades have various tangs, which is the part the handle fastens to, usually two types of guards, and some knives are even made without a guard. There are many methods of finishing the handle or butt cap, and a full-tang knife, just to confuse things, does not have a butt cap.

The most important parts of a knife are, of course, the blade and the handle. The sharpened portion of the blade is called, simply, the edge. The back of the blade, or that section that is unsharpened opposite the edge, is the back or spine. The blade has a point, naturally, and that portion up the back opposite the tip is referred to as the false edge. If it is sharpened, it is called a swedge. The curves and grinds on the back, particularly if the knife is a benchmade type, are bevels, and if they are well executed, they will add to the beauty of the blade. On some knives there will be a slight inward curve on that part of the blade just under the guard, and it is called a choil, finger clip, or finger cutout. For the expert knifeman it allows the placement of the first or second finger down the back of the blade for greater control of the knife when skinning game or caping trophy specimens about the head, where extreme caution must be exercised.

That small section of metal just under the guard, which the choil or finger-

Professional knifemaker Howard Viele marks the steel blank after painting it with Bykem steel blue. A meter scriber is used to scratch the outline of the pattern on the surface.

How the outline appears on the blank.

Rough metal files are used to remove excess metal and to profile the blade.

Rough-filing the blade down to shape.

clip sometimes cuts into, is known as the ricasso. This is the place many custom craftsmen or commercial cutlers favor for placing their names. Even the guard may be complicated to the novice. Its use, basically, is to prevent the hand from slipping down onto the blade and being cut. The bits of metal extending from the guard are known as quillions, and most hunting knives will have one quillion—the shorter the better. Fighting and boot knives will have two, and these are to protect the hand when using the knife in combat.

What is held in the hand is the handle or grip, and this comes in several types, too. A full handle, that is, completely covering the tang, is known as a narrow-tang or stick-handle knife. When the tang extends to the very width of the blade, it is known as a full-tang knife. Usually, the stick-handle knife is made more decorative by the use of spacers, which do little except add to the attractiveness of the overall picture, and a butt cap of brass (which can be heavy), nickle silver, aluminum, or stainless steel. Some stick-handle knives don't even use butt caps, and this is a matter of preference of the maker. Some knives don't even have guards, which the maker may feel add weight to the knife, and a small choil is placed on the handle to give a solid grip. There isn't much left on the handle except an escutcheon plate, which may be placed in the center of the handle. This is a nice touch and allows the owner to place a bit of engraving, name or initials, on the knife.

But we're not through yet, since the tangs of knives must be discussed to give a complete understanding of knife terminology. On stick-handle knives the tang may be round, half-round, or extend to the very end of the handle, where it will be taken up with a threaded nut. It can be flat or half-flat, where it will be held by both epoxy and rivets. A full-tang knife is one where the tang is the thickness and width of the blade. There are also brass or nickle silver–wrapped full tangs that usually cost more when ordered from a craftsman. The full tang may also be tapered, which shows a distinctive touch, exhibits the skills of the maker, and lightens the knife.

As to the construction of a knife, the full tang may be easier where the metal is covered with slabs or scales of various material held with industrial epoxy and rivets. When arguments arise among knifemakers, there are heated discussions as to which type of knife is stronger. Each has its proponents, and if the tang is cut wide enough where it enters the handle, a stick-handle knife will be as strong as a full-tang knife. Both are really exercises in design elements of the overall knife, and both make attractive knives.

One fairly innovative method of construction is the inter-frame devised by Jimmy Lile a few years ago. This is a full-tang knife with the center of the steel handle cut out to accept various materials. Again, this is an exercise in knife-making skill and, while it does add to the beauty of a knife, may be too difficult for the beginner to attempt.

Now that most of this is out of the way, and the reader is thoroughly confused, let's move on to a couple of hints. Don't make the guard too large. If the quillion extends too far, it will only make the knife awkward to use, especially if the sportsman is working inside the cavity of a large animal. That's one reason many expert knife users prefer a small choil to keep the hand secure when handling a knife. The butt cap or pommel is usually made from the same material as the guard since they complement each other. While brass is easier to work, it will also tarnish faster and, of course, will add weight to the knife.

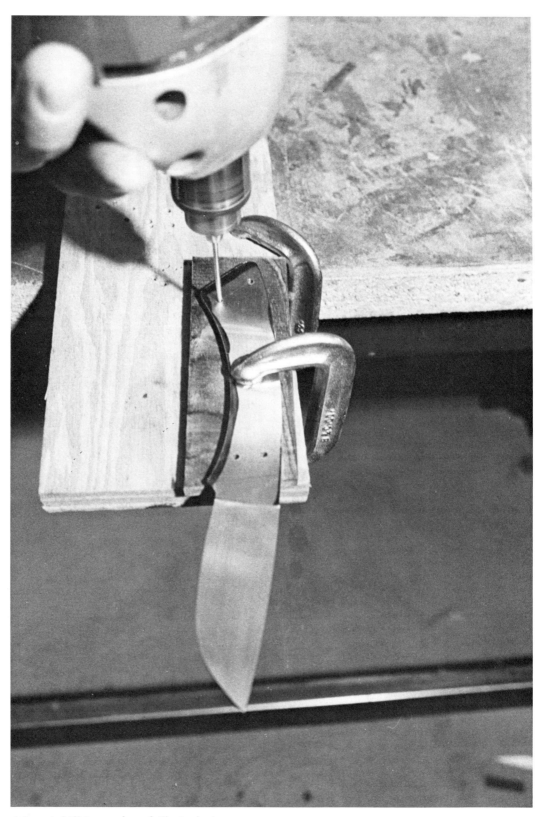

A hand drill is used to drill pin holes.

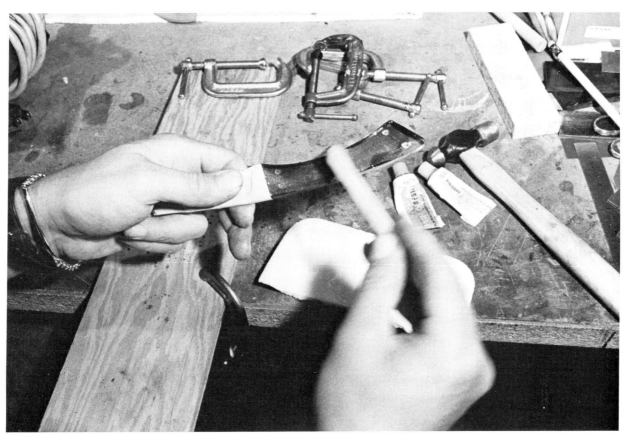

Applying epoxy for the handle slabs.

Place the pins in the holes and clamp everything tight. At this point the pins are peened down, with the head of the pin to be filed off during the finishing of the handle.

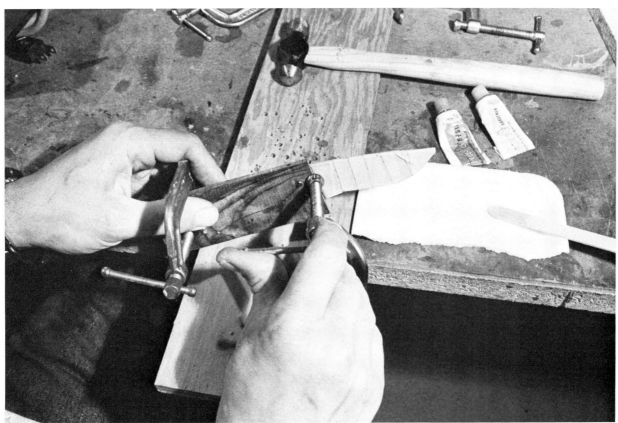

Rough-filing of the handle.

Fine finishing of the blade. All polishing is done with successively finer grits of wet or dry emery paper. Begin with a 60 grit, then 220, 320, and, finally, 400. Remember to change the direction of your stroke each time the grit is changed.

Knifemaker Howard Viele examines a knife for flaws.

Nickle silver is handsome and some makers, like Rod Chappel, frequently use stainless steel. Many knifemakers don't even use spacers on their knives, although this should be left to the artful proclivities of the craftsman. Spacers can be made from a wide range of material: plastic, bone, stag, wood, and a wide range of metals. D'Alton Holder uses large circles of amber combined with other contrasting materials, and some makers use jade. Spacers will add beauty to a knife, make it unique, and depending on the materials used, even add a bit of value. To a more practical end, they work as washers and permit the maker to obtain a proper fit. However, if the handle section is cut properly for length and fit, there will be no need for spacers.

Keep in mind that a simple design is best, and all unnecessary ingredients should be eliminated until the aspiring craftsman has gained control of his tools and materials.

3 || CHOOSING THE RIGHT STEEL

It has frequently been said that steel is the heart of a knife. That's true enough, but heat-treating is what gives a piece of steel a heart and soul, too. The newcomer to knifemaking may be confused about steels, just as confused as some of the professional knifemen who continually argue the merits of certain steels. Oddly enough, this is a valid argument because it depends on what the knifemaker, and eventual user, wants in a blade.

Some knifemakers are also hunters, and this gives them an advantage toward knowing what a blade should do in the field. To some, the greatest accomplishment in knifemaking is long edge-holding, while others insist on ease of sharpening, and many more will want their knife to remain in pristine condition as long as it is used. Unfortunately, not all these advantages can be found in one knife blade. If a man wants hardness in a knife, he may have to sacrifice edge holding, and the sportsman who wants rust resistance plus edge holding would probably prefer a blade of rust-resistant steel such as 154-CM, 440-C, or Stellite 6-K, which isn't steel at all. But if any of these high-chromium-content alloys are used, it will be found that they are extremely difficult to sharpen, particularly in the field, making the user's task more difficult.

All alloys used for knifemaking have a predetermined range for each particular steel when being heat-treated, and it is this heat range that gives steel its guts. For example, a knifemaker (who shall be nameless, to save him from further embarrassment) ran some tests a few years back after making a batch of knives from various popular knife steels, all with a Rockwell hardness of 59 on the C scale. Bob Loveless's observation on this operation was that giving each piece of steel the same Rockwell hardness showed a critical lack of knowledge of steels. It is true, since each type of steel will work best as a knife blade with an already predicted hardness.

What most knifemakers offer are steels that will have varying degrees of strength, hardness, and rust resistance. Many knifemakers offer a variety of steels, while others, such as Bob Loveless and George Herron, use 154-CM exclusively—although Bob is fascinated with Stellite 6-K and continues to experiment with it. But for the reader to grasp more easily the intricacies of steel, let's discuss Rockwell hardness for a bit.

Actually, "Rockwelling" a blade is a fairly simple process of indenting the heat-treated blade with a tip known as the Brale diamond point. There are also a number of scales on the Rockwell tester, but only the C scale is used for knife steels. The finished blade is placed under the tip on a flat surface; then a lever is brought forward until the tip makes a slight indention in the steel. The first lever throw brings a 10-kilogram weight into play; then, as the lever is moved, it applies 150 kilograms. The difference between the two weights or pressures is read directly off the C scale. What the Rockwell test accomplishes is that the read-out will give the blade maker the information that it has been heat-treated properly for that particular piece of steel.

Arguments abound, as with everything else in knifemaking, that the Rockwell reading just tells the hardness of that one section of blade where it was tested, usually the ricasso—but what about the rest of the blade? Experienced knifemen can be pretty confident, after using a certain heat-treating plant over a period of time, that their blades will be properly treated and be of the correct hardness over the entire blade.

But to go back to the beginning—what is steel? Iron with other ingredients added in various percentages to give special qualities that the knifemaker wants to give his customers. It is doubtful if more than a handful of people realize that over 100 million tons of steel are produced annually in the United States and the American knifemaker uses less than 1 percent of that. Even all the kits and blades sold account for a minuscule amount of the stuff, and prime steels, which can be compared to fine cognacs, are used by knifemakers, including the talented amateur. Tool steels that are melted, poured, and rolled with special care and precision end up in the blades of sportsmen used in the high mountains of the West, the plains of Africa, and just about any place else you care to name.

Tool steels are made as any other steel, but it is the percentage of other elements that give it special properties. F-8 could be considered a fairly simple steel, since it contains only carbon, tungsten, and chromium in varying percentages. M-2 might be called a more complicated steel, since it has nine alloys, all adding different things to the finished steel. For example, tungsten gives a finer grain structure, manganese helps with hardness and wear resistance, nickle gives it strength and toughness, and silicon will also add toughness and hardness. Chromium gives the finished blade its ability to accept a high polish plus wear resistance and toughness. Molybdenum also adds some of the characteristics of both chromium and tungsten. The interaction of all these alloys will give the knife its desired properties—if the blades are properly heat-treated. The realm of steel-making is complex indeed; yet the novice knifeman need not be a trained metallurgist in order to proceed, since he will be buying bars of steel already mixed and poured and sometimes heat-treated.

Most steels have a sort of coding arrangement that gives the user a hint of the type of steel and the method used for hardening. Water-hardening steels are identified by the letter W, as with W-1, W-2; O indicates an oil-hardening steel;

and A stands for air-hardening. The letter D is for die steels, and M is for molybdenum-based types. This is not a complete list of all the steels available, and for those who want to delve into the technical aspects of steel, there is nothing better than *Tool Steels,* by Roberts, Hamaker, and Johnson, published by the American Society for Metals, Metals Park, Ohio. The book is regarded as a bible of tool steels among serious knifemakers, and well-thumbed copies will be found in every good knife shop.

It will be useful here to give the reader the opportunity of glancing over a list of ingredients of the more popular knife steels.

154-CM	Carbon	1.05
	Manganese	0.60
	Phosphorus	0.030
	Sulfur	0.030
	Silicon	0.25
	Chromium	14.00
	Molybdenum	4.00
440-C	Carbon	1.00
	Manganese	0.50
	Silicon	0.40
	Chromium	17.05
	Molybdenum	0.45
	Nickle	0.20
F-8	Carbon	1.30
	Tungsten	8.00
	Chromium	4.00
	Vanadium	0.25
D-2	Carbon	1.50
	Manganese	0.25/0.40
	Silicon	0.30/0.50
	Chromium	11.50
	Molybdenum	1.00
	Vanadium	0.90
W-2	Carbon	0.06/1.4
	Manganese	0.25
	Silicon	0.25
	Vanadium	0.25
M-2	Carbon	0.85
	Manganese	0.25
	Phosphorus	0.00 (0.03 max.)
	Sulfur	0.00 (0.03 max.)
	Silicon	0.30
	Chromium	4.20
	Molybdenum	5.00
	Tungsten	6.35
	Vanadium	1.90

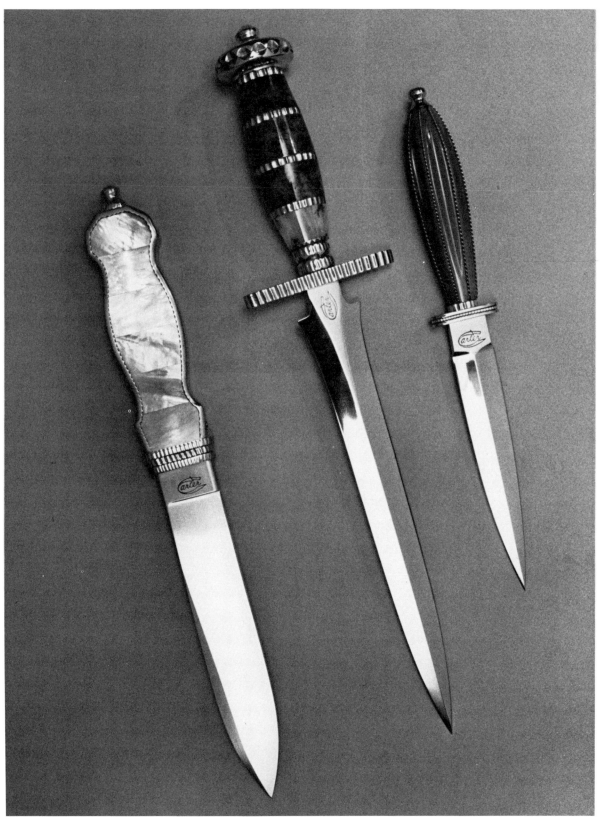

Three fine show knives by Fred Carter. The handle materials are (left to right) mother-of-pearl, amber, and polished Dahl sheep horn.

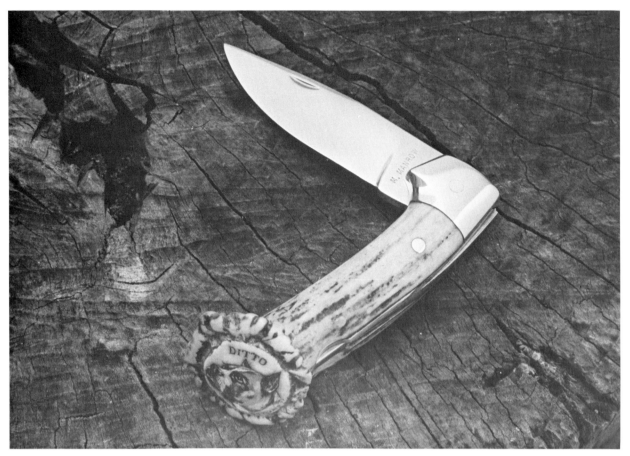

A folder by Mike Manrow with crown stag scrimshawed by Glen Stearns.

A-2	Carbon	1.00
	Manganese	0.50/0.70
	Silicon	0.25/0.40
	Chromium	5.00
	Molybdenum	1.00
O-1	Carbon	0.90
	Tungsten	0.50
	Manganese	1.35
	Silicon	0.35
	Chromium	0.50

There is one other material used by some knifemakers that is not a steel at all but a wrought product, almost like a tool steel, but receiving its properties through chemistry. This is known as Stellite Number 6-K. It is manufactured, concocted, or crafted by the Stellite Division of the Cabot Corporation. It is a cobalt alloy and extremely hard. Its rust resistance is five times greater than either 440-C or 154-CM, and its resistance to wear is better than 10 to 20 times greater than most properly hardened tool steels, even though it is put into use at a low Rockwell hardness—47. Although relatively new for knife blades, this product has been around for over 20 years and was developed for use where it was necessary to have a very hard material to cut tool steels. One superb knifemaker, Mike Franklin, is using it exclusively, but he confesses that it is extremely hard to work and even more difficult to sharpen. In fact, Franklin recommends the use of the Eze-Lap sharpening tool or "steel," which has a synthetic diamond surface.

Let's take a look at the composition of Stellite 6-K.

Carbon	1.5/1.9
Manganese	2.00
Tungsten	3.5/5.5
Silicon	2.00
Chromium	28.00/32.00
Molybdenum	1.05
Nickle	3.09

It can easily be seen that if 154-CM has 14 percent chromium, and 440-C has 17.05 percent chromium, Stellite 6-K, with 28 percent and over, must be pretty hard. Franklin admits to using more sanding belts and other expendable items for it than for any other steel. In spite of its high chromium content, which should enable 6-K to be polished with ease, it just is not that simple to obtain a high mirror finish. Added to the difficulty in working with this material is its high price—about $18 per pound at this writing. In fact, Franklin and a few others who are trying this formulation for knives have to charge a premium price. Because of its high resistance to abrasions and corrosion, many consider this the ultimate material for a knife blade. However, it should not be considered by the novice knifemaker because there will be enough problems working with easier steels.

Now we'll look at some knifemakers' reactions to other steels. Once the craftsman has gone beyond the kit stage and wants to start with a regular piece of steel, what should he use? And should he heat-treat the blade himself or have it done by a professional shop? It should be noted that most craftsmen have the steel heat-treated at outside companies that have the ability and equipment to do a proper job. It takes highly specialized skills, including trained metallurgists, to heat-treat to near-finished dimensions. A knife blade when it is ready for heat-treating is ground very thin compared to other pieces of metal and requires special atmospheres such as salt or oil baths to complete the task properly. Cryogenic treatment, that is, freezing the blades at certain stages, requires equipment that will bring the steel down to temperatures of 120°F and will hold *exactly* at that range for hours or longer. Both 440-C and 154-CM are often cryogenically treated in this subzero quench to ensure greater hardness.

There are a few knifemakers who do their own heat-treating, and they do successful work. The Nolen brothers of Texas had their oven built by a couple of friends at NASA in Houston, received proper instructions for its use, and turn out fine knives at the correct Rockwell hardness for the particular steel they are using. Of course, one of the great frustrations of knifemakers is the warp aspect of certain steels when they are heat-treated. Usually, the professional knifeman will send a dozen or more blades to the shop at one time, since charges are based on weight rather than by the piece. Certain steels do have a greater proclivity for warping than others. Corbet Sigman has used W-2 because he claims it delivers very clean bars from his supplier, but he believes that if he make a blade longer than 5 inches, it will warp very badly in the quench. For anything longer than 5 inches he uses O-1. But the hazards are not all past. Although W-2 will harden at high temperatures, it must be drawn (tempered) to avoid brittleness. More often than not, it will break into pieces when it hits the brine. It can be pretty discouraging watch-

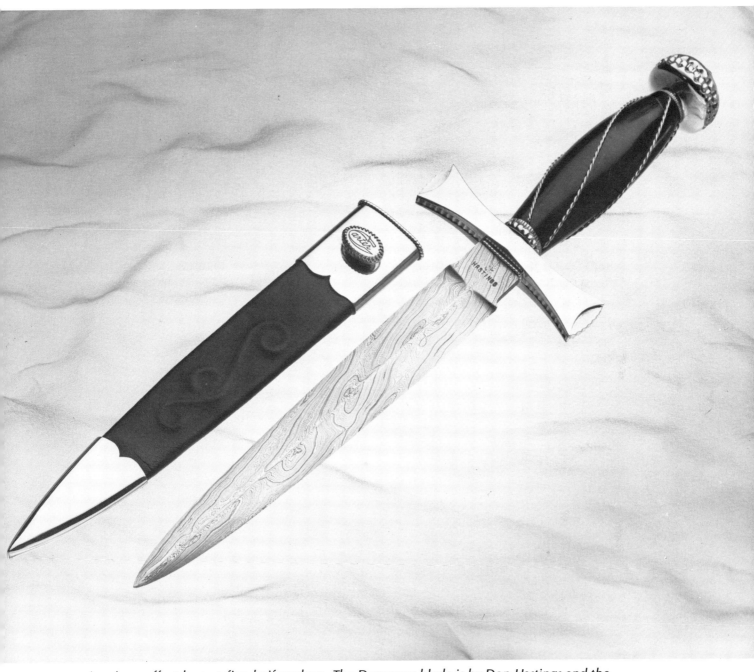

A unique effort by two fine knifemakers. The Damascus blade is by Don Hastings and the handle and sheath by Fred Carter. The blade is 8 inches long, and the German silver sheath is of ebony and silver plus silver wire wrapped about the handle.

(Opposite) A matching dagger and bowie knife by master craftsman Buster Warenski with abalone handles and silver sheaths. Note the engraving on the guard.

ing hours of labor disintegrate while you think of a couple of funny stories . . . to keep from crying.

O-1 steel is found in most knifemakers' shops and is considered a pretty good steel for beginners. It will grind easily and quench in almost any oil, and more important, is reasonably inexpensive compared to the more exotic grades. But O-1 really is not a quality steel any more than W-2 is, and both will rust badly after use. A step up the ladder for the craftsman might be A-2, which has a reasonable amount of chromium and gives both fairly good edge-holding and some corrosion resistance. But even the famous in knifemakers are always experimenting. Take Ted Dowell, a top maker from Bend, Oregon. In an earlier catalog his steels were listed as F-8, D-2, and 440-C. In catalog 6, issued in 1976, he changed his steels to D-2, 440-C, and 154-CM—eliminating the F-8. Dowell is an experienced sportsman, having hunted game over most of the West and Alaska. He has tested in the field such steels as O-1, A-2, A-8, A-10, D-2, D-3, D-7, L-6, F-8, S-5, S-5 modified, W-1, M-2, M-3 type 1, Vasco B-B, 1095, 5160, 1060, 440-C, Versasteel, Graph-Tung, and 154-CM. Having once been a mathematics professor, Dowell has a technical turn of mind, and he made a field-grade knife from each of these steels treated to the proper degree of hardness. Over the years, he took each knife into the field for proper testing. Dowell says, "Hardness is no index to edge-holding, and hardness and toughness do not guarantee superior edge-holding. I have nothing against high hardness, but in my experience good edge-holding has never been directly related to high hardness." Of the steels Ted now offers his customers, he has this to say: "D-2 is the edge-holder, and 440-C and 154-CM are included as superior stainless steels where a high degree of corrosion resistance is desired. My recommendation regarding blade steels is this: D-2 if you want a 'using' knife blade with superior edge-holding qualities if you don't plan to use it around salt water. For the collector, 154-CM or 440-C. Also, if you plan to use the knife near salt water, the stainless steels are a better choice."

Recently, Dowell has had some success working with a new steel called Vasco Wear. Dowell recently said, "This steel has some truly remarkable qualities to offer for its use as a knife blade. For instance, it substantially betters my long-time favorite D-2 in two categories: toughness and wear resistance. This steel is one-and-a-half times as tough as D-2 and has *twice* the wear resistance at Rockwell 60." However, the one meaningful test of any knife steel is to make a couple of blades and use them. This Dowell has done and still remains impressed. He went on, "This is a great knife steel although not stainless, about like D-2 for its stain resistance, it takes a somewhat dull polish, but it does have all kinds of toughness and the edge wears and wears and wears." Dowell admits that Vasco Wear is a tough steel to work and for that reason charges an extra $50 for blades crafted of that particular steel.

Incidentally, since Dowell brought it up, now is a good time to pass on some words regarding the so-called stainless steels. The term "stainless" is somewhat of a misnomer and it would be better if such steels were referred to as corrosion resistant or rust resistant. All steels will eventually stain, particularly if used in or around corrosion-inducing climes or touched by blood and other body fluids of animals. The high chromium content of 440-C, 154-CM, and even Stellite 6-K will certainly aid in keeping blades crafted of these materials in original condition longer than any other blade. Loveless has said some skin-diver knives made of

154-CM have been used extensively along the California coast without showing signs of corrosion or pitting. This does not mean that subjecting such knives to careless use will guarantee long life. Even these blades, when used in or around salt water, should be washed off promptly after use and coated with a light layer of oil.

What other steels are popular among knifemakers? Billy Mace Imel offers three: A-2, D-2, and 440-C. The blades of his folding knives are usually crafted of 154-CM. Harold Corby offers two steels from the same family—440-C and 154-CM—and Buster Warenski, the knife artist from Richfield, Utah, does the same. Californian Dave Cosby emulates Bob Loveless and is loyal to 154-CM. Cosby feels that 154-CM offers both qualities of a good knife: a superior edge-holding capability and excellent corrosion resistance. While admitting there is no such thing as the perfect knife steel, Cosby says, "154-CM is as close to it as is currently obtainable."

Perhaps a final controversy over knife steels should be discussed in brief—the argument regarding forging versus the more modern method of stock removal. The majority of knifemakers use the latter technique, which, in George Herron's words, means "Taking a bar of steel and grinding away everything that doesn't look like a knife and you have a knife." Perhaps that's too simple an explanation, but basically that's what it's all about.

With steel mills delivering fine steels already rolled into practically any size the maker could desire, why should he forge? To many it is a return to the traditional craftwork of an earlier America, where the song of the blacksmith's hammer rang through every village and the sparks flew like a daily Fourth of July.

Forging dates back to long before Christ and was the method used to craft the tridents and blades of the Roman gladiators. Heavy hammers pounded out the swords and lances of the Crusaders, the axes of the Vikings, the delicate rapiers of the musketeers, and the cutlasses of buccaneers. Even the blades of our own men of history showed the hammer marks of the men who forged them. Jim Bridger, Jedediah Smith, and the entire passel of mountain men carried forged blades from the early factories of Sheffield, and perhaps the most famous blade of all, the Bowie knife, was forged by the legendary James Black long years ago in Washington, Arkansas.

The modern knifemakers who continue to forge do it for a number of reasons. Some feel that the mill rollers impart a directional quality to the grain of the steel and they reforge to move this grain in one direction. Bill Moran forges, of course, since he must gain the structure of the Damascus pattern, and no mill can do that for him. Others, like Bo Randall, forge because they feel it makes a better blade, and Randall admits that he wants to deliver a blade crafted in the traditional manner. Corbet Sigman uses both methods and, when pressed for an answer, admits that both methods are good if done by a competent craftsman. Dan Dennehy is another fine knifemaker who uses both methods of crafting a blade, forging the steel for his longer blades and using the stock-removal technique on smaller knives. The blacksmith no doubt has a more difficult task because he is constantly working his metal by heating it in a forge. As the steel is heated, it continually changes color from light straw to darkened brown to blue tones and shades of red to orange and finally to white when it becomes molten. These changes of color take place as the temperature rises or falls, and the blacksmith must be constantly alert in order to hammer the blade when the color is precisely right. The grain structure is also altered by forging, so that it runs true to the cutting edge of the finished blade. The master blacksmiths can also do what is known as "packing," in which the blade, when almost completed, is rapidly hammered with light blows at a low heat. This compacts the fibers of the steel. When the forging is almost completed, the blade is hammered to shape. Then the blade is sanded and the cutting bevel is set in; it is hardened and hammered again by reheating, all under the watchful eye of the artisan.

The blacksmith's blade has been going through a process of tempering all the time, and now the final task is taken up. Rather than send the blade off to a commercial house, as do the stock-removal proponents, for heat-treating in an electric furnace, the smith tempers the blade with a hand-held acetylene torch, slowly tempering the back to a certain hardness, shading various colors through the center of the blade, and finally just touching the edge and point. This gives the blade greater resilience in the center, makes the back fairly soft for toughness, and gives the cutting edge the maximum amount of hardness to hold sharpness. Thus, the smith can accomplish more in a blade by giving it differing amounts of hardness where necessary. Those who are good at tempering certainly may consider their forged blades the royalty of the knife world.

Unfortunately, those less skilled can forge in more flaws than necessary and end up with some pretty sorry blades. The constant heating, hammering, and reheating is a lot of work, but for someone who enjoys the smithy's anvil, and if the neighbors don't complain, this may be the choice. Otherwise, the accepted method of grinding away steel until a knife remains, either by filing by hand or by using modern machines, will probably lead to success a lot faster.

With either method bear in mind that there is no free ride with steel; every choice is a compromise between easier fabrication, the appearance of the finished blade, or various characteristics of those qualities known as hardness, edge holding, abrasion, and corrosion resistance. A steel that gives known advantages in one or more areas will have faults in others. In sum, there is no perfect steel. To compound the mystery further, then, what makes one expert rave about a particular steel while another cutler takes the opposite tack? One man's opinion, mostly. The new knife craftsman who aspires to the perfect blade can do no better than select his favorite knifemaker and, if he likes what the man turns out, use the same steel for his first efforts. The steels used by quality makers will deliver a better knife than anything the new man has ever used before, particularly if the new maker's only comparison is with early commercially produced knives. Once the kit stage has been passed, single blanks of most of the steels mentioned are available from many of the knifemaker supply houses. The tried-and-true method is to use the knife in the field; then, if it does not deliver what was expected—and only then—try another alloy.

The question of Magnafluxing blades should be mentioned. For the uninitiated, this is a method of finding faults or fractures in steel and is widely used in the firearms and automotive fields. No commercial cutlery firm to my knowledge uses this expensive and time-consuming process, and certainly no bench-made knife is subjected to such complex testing. A couple of knifemakers have said they occasionally do Magnaflux, and this is possible if they have a gunmaker friend nearby. But after conversations with them, doubts remain. After all, a knife is not as hazardous to use as an automobile or firearm, and the worst that can happen is that the blade will break. With proper construction and correct heat-treatment, even this is practically unknown among knife users.

Commercially, heat-treated blades are the norm for most craftsmen, and the novice knifemaker should not, at this stage, consider doing it himself. There are many excellent commerical firms around the country (listed in the back of the book), and these have been selected for the consistent reports from the many craftsmen using their facilities. A quality heat-treating firm will enhance the skills of the craftsman, but a first-rate heat treatment won't do anything for an inferior steel and a bad heat treatment won't help a good steel.

To obtain quality in your first handmade knife, and leaving skilled craftsmanship aside for the moment, select a good steel and an experienced heat-treating outfit. Then half the battle will be won.

4

ALL ABOUT HANDLES

The handle of a knife is one of the few places a knifeman can exercise his artistic ability with a full range of both practical and exotic materials. Almost all the old-time knives, even those from Europe, had handles or slabs of Sambar stag. This was the traditional knifemaker's material since it was beautiful as well as practical. Stag was sturdy, and the roughened side gave fine grasping qualities in the hand. A few years ago, however, the Indian government placed an embargo on the export of Sambar stag because the animals were being exterminated by poachers who wanted a big part of the stag market. The government also declared that the stag could not be exported unless it was worked by the Indians themselves. Naturally, this would not do for anyone crafting a made-to-fit handle on a benchmade knife; so other materials had to be found. Stag is still obtainable in small quantities, and a few of the supply firms listed may even have some at this writing. Other animal horns are also good, and whitetail and mule deer horn will work, although the cores can be rather soft and spongy. Crown stag is exceptionally handsome where the antler flares out, and it makes a good handle.

Leather was once popular, but after hard use it becomes unattractive, washers shrink, and it absorbs blood and body fluids from the game being dressed out. The late Harry Morseth devised a means of impregnating leather that practically guarantees the life of a knife crafted by Morseth.

Bone is another excellent material, and although not as popular as it once was, it makes good-looking handles. Ivory has become so expensive it has almost been priced out of the market. Ivory was always an extra-cost item on benchmade knives, and a few years ago the premium was around $5 to $15. Now some custom craftsmen have posted prices of $50 extra for an ivory-handled knife. This is not surprising because ivory has jumped from $18 per pound to the most recent price of $40—and that's unsorted ivory found on the ground in Africa. There is no doubt that ivory will add to the beauty of a quality knife as it slowly ages and takes on golden tones, but there is a problem with ivory, too. While it is definitely not a suitable material for a practical working knife, it has advantages on collector's pieces. But even on finely crafted knives it has a proclivity to check and crack, and although a few fine hairlines may add character to a handle, deep cracks that catch a thumbnail aren't that attractive. Why some ivory should crack is not fully understood. For example, carved antique ivory objets d'art from India or China with unblemished surfaces are often found in museums. Old ivory stocks on some ancient oriental firearms are as good as new, and modern ivory-carved pistol grips by Alvin White or John Suth remain as they did on the carver's bench. In fact, some craftsmen feel that may be the answer—hand carving. Lloyd Hale has said the one big problem with shaping ivory is that no high-speed machines should be used since the heat generated will cause structural changes in the material.

Knifemaker Bob Dozier says that daily applications of a fine mineral oil or baby oil to ivory handles will prevent cracking. This must be done daily for at least six months. The other problem is that even if the handle slabs are hand carved, the heat generated by the drying epoxy may cause damage. Often the heat will go as high as 300°F, and with the ivory held by pins and rivets, it will be constantly twisting and moving as the epoxy sets and dries.

Other materials that have a tendency to crack are buffalo horn and ebony. Both Gaboon and Macassar ebony are equally bad in resisting shrinkage. While buffalo horn does make beautiful jet-black handles, it will eventually crack and split.

The most popular woods are those imported from South America, Africa, and Southeast Asia. When properly finished and polished, they have a beauty that rivals the most artfully crafted knife. Cocobolo, teak, rosewood, Australian brushbox, concalo alves, pau ferrau, lignum vitae, European walnut, and a host of other exotic woods make fine handles. Many of these woods also contain natural oils that give a sheen and help protect the wood from cracking.

Woods indigenous to the United States are also popular with knifemakers. Native woods such as persimmon, cherry, oak, maple, osage orange, mesquite, and cholla cactus have all been used for knife handles.

Many knifemakers like to combine exotic and unusual materials to create interesting-looking knives. Horace Wiggins likes to use certain diseased woods for their unusual patterns. He is also famed for being the first to use cactus impregnated with colored epoxies for knife handles, and has even been known to mix up a batch of clear epoxy with tiny sea shells to create a handle of strong and unusual beauty.

Bob Oleson is a comparatively new knifemaker from California and does impressive knives and small daggers and dirks in the style of the old San Francisco makers Will & Finck and Michael Price. Oleson emulates these old-timers with beautifully crafted handles of abalone shell inlaid into nickle silver handles. He is also known to work with mother-of-pearl, and the influence of the California coast seems to have given Oleson direction.

Among the rarest of materials is jade, and this has been used by a number of craftsmen. Before he gave up knifemaking, Gil Hibben was living in Alaska and used native jade in considerable amounts for his extra-fancy knives. Since the material is so difficult to cut, it demands specialized equipment and skills. Jade is not inexpensive either, and the most recent quote was $3,000 on a Dowell integral-hilt and cap knife. Alaskan jade runs the gamut of green tones, and from Wyoming comes black jade. One knifeman, Ralph Combs of Naples, Florida, has recently turned to jade after purchasing his own diamond-cutting wheels and crafts some exceptional knives with the handsome material. His prices are considerably less than $3,000.

Baltic amber is popular with some craftsmen. This is another high-priced material and is usually combined with rare woods, ebony, or ivory. It makes a striking handle, but is best used on presentation pieces.

Perhaps the most unusual of all is ossik, and for many years sportsmen visiting Alaska wanted a couple of small ossiks to use as cocktail stirrers (the monster-sized specimens hung on the wall). What is ossik? The family jewels or pride and joy of the walrus. Not only does it make fine knife handles, but a good conversation piece, too. Highly polished, it has tones of brown and gold flecks running to the surface. Like ivory, ossik will check and should be treated gently. As with other rarities, ossik isn't cheap. The last time I priced it in the shops of Anchorage an 18-inch ossik ran about $200. Certainly large enough for sufficient knife handles to last a lifetime. However, if the novice knifemaker demands the exotic for a handle, a couple of knifemaking buddies could share expenses.

All of these materials have been nature's products, but everything from stainless steel self-handled knives to imitation materials have been used, including some interesting results from the chemist's test tube. Once upon a time, bone was gouged and routed out to simulate stag. Delrin was and is popular and much used by many commercial knifemakers in this country. Other materials are hard rubber, celluloid, and various plastics. The most popular modern material is Micarta, developed by Westinghouse. It is a phenolic resin and was originally intended for coverings on tables and countertops. We won't even try to guess the first knifemaker who used this on knives, but it was a huge success. It is generally accepted that Micarta makes the best handle of all. Bob Loveless says that linen or fabric Micarta is the standard handle slab material on Loveless knives, and that's a pretty good accolade from the master. Micarta is available in a range of colors, including a paper Micarta with the texture and tone of tusk ivory. There are now wood-impregnated Micartas that come in cocobolo, rosewood, and others. Ted Dowell says, "I would place linen-based Micarta at the very top of the list for durability in knife handle material." Bone Micarta (a laminate of paper and epoxy) closely resembles ivory but will not check. Scrimshanders have taken to Micarta and turn out some first-class work. This does not mean that these men do not use other materials—they do. Loveless admits to using Sambar stag on his own knives because he likes the "stuff" but points out that it isn't as strong or stable as Micarta and can warp and shrink. A knifemaker with Loveless's capabilities has no trouble changing a handle when its appearance begins to suffer.

Corbet Sigman goes along with Micartas, too. "The laminated phenolics of linen- and canvas-based Micartas are highest in durability, and I highly recommend them if a knife is to be put into daily use."

Some Micartas are even laminated with different colors and give the appearance of an ocean swirl viewed from a high-flying aircraft.

But this is not the last word on handle materials. Some enterprising fel-

A variety of shape, form, and size. (Left to right) An all-steel knife with thumb serration and choil on the handle by Track Knives; a fine shape by Corbet Sigman of rosewood; a new model by Track Knives of ivory Micarta and decorative pins; a straight-blade (although it resembles a folder) stag-handled sheath knife by Frank Centofante; and a handsome small knife by Howard Viele.

lows have used snakeskin tightly sewn along the bottom of the handle and then impregnated with various epoxies. Others have tried animal hides, and one imaginative lad even braids colored leather strips in the manner of the gauchos.

Whatever man or nature has created has probably, at one time or another, been used for the handle of a knife. Should the craftsman's bank account be sufficient, even rare jewels or gold and silver may be used in emulation of the old maharajas of India. Even Gerber has used ice agate and jade on the handles of some of their specially crafted presentation folders. Many of the knifemaker's supply shops will, on occasion, have some of the more exotic materials on hand, but depending on the scarcity of the item, the price may jump with the regularity of the stock market when the bulls are running.

In all probability, the most important factor for the beginner will be achieving a practical, good-looking handle. There are various finger grips, rings, lumps, bumps, and grooves that put the hand in the proper position. But the question arises: What is the proper position for using a knife?

Handles can be more of a problem for the knifemaker than most people realize. There is such a thing as a proper fit, and when most knives are grasped or tried for size, they are usually held only one way. What the prospective knife user seldom appreciates is that the knife will constantly be moved in the hand. At times

(Left to right) A finely crafted hunter made by Horace Wiggins, of seashells embedded in epoxy and finger grooves; a stag-handled hunter by Gray Taylor; the High Country with a cutout in the handle for lightness and Micarta slabs by George Stone; and a small ivory-handled model by Frank Vought.

it will be turned upside down in order to cut upward; it will also be used in a straight up-and-down sawing motion; and working blind inside an animal, it will be held in almost any position imaginable. Which leads us naturally to a discussion of finger grips. Some men may like a custom-fitted handle where the finger grips lead the complexities of the hand into the proper position. Well, this is great if the knife is used only one way, but after a while it will become so uncomfortable that the user will want to toss the offending blade into a deep snowbank.

Many craftsmen and their customers equate the comfort of target grips on a handgun to finger grips on a knife. But it doesn't work that way. Once a target handgun is set in the hand, it does not change position. A knife, if properly used, is in constant motion if the sportsman wants to have full use of the blade. To overcome this, some makers will use a few finger grooves on the handle; others call anything that interferes with the movement of the hand an abomination. Advice? Leave finger grips alone until experience is gained in crafting and using knives. Then, if there must be something on the handle, start with a slight choil. It will give some added comfort, allow good hand movement, and won't be too uncomfortable in all those odd and strange positions a knife will be used in.

The size of the handle is equally important and size is a subject to which little thought is given. Few realize that a knife handle can be too small and yet be

50

perfect. In particular, this applies to small daggers or boot knives, where the handle in some is just long enough to be placed against the palm. Yet such a length would be impractical for a sportsman's knife. Even on the latter a handle can be too long and get in the way. Take a caping knife used to skin the cape of an animal and to be worked around the mouth and eyes of game. The handle should not be too long, since the delicate blade will be maneuvered by fingertip control in all those hard-to-get-at places.

On the other hand, Rod Chappel, who crafts some of the most graceful knives extant, belies the argument with sweeping curves and zooming angles on both his blades and handles. Chappel's knives are a designer's dream, and they come alive each time they are turned and viewed from another angle. Oddly enough, they are also easy to use and, in spite of the various curves on the handle, the knife can be used in many positions—all comfortable. Chappel has his critics, who say that his knives are too wild. Yet his admirers, and I am one of a large group, see a great deal of beauty in a Chappel knife.

But to the more practical side of handles for the novice. A block of wood or Micarta placed diagonally across the palm will give a reasonably good idea of fit. If it extends beyond 1/4 inch, don't be too concerned. The handle should not be perfectly round, since it will be constantly turning in the hand. An oval or flat form is better, and it will be easier to grasp the knife. Should the new knifemaker care to experiment, the realization will soon come that the closed hand is full of little bumps and hollows. Some knifemakers will grind slight mounds and ridges in various parts of the handle to conform to a better fit. It makes no difference if the first knife is to be a stick-handle or full-tang; the same considerations of comfort and fit must be kept in mind.

As to blade length, this is more a personal consideration than anything else. Naturally someone who lives and hunts in the Far West or Alaska might want a slightly longer blade to handle larger game. Those who live in the eastern part of our country and seldom go after anything larger than whitetail deer or a small bear might want a shorter blade. Fashions in knives change slower than clothing or cars, but change they do, and a few years ago we saw a trend to the short-bladed knife. Many sportsmen who want a comfortable knife to carry all day long usually opt for something around 3 inches or, perhaps, even 3½ inches. Long blades, meaning those of 7 to 12 inches, are out, and can mark the outlander as a neophyte as quickly as appearing with the wrong-gauge gun for grouse shooting or showing up on a trout stream with a bait-casting rig. To find out why this is so, we'll have to go back a few years. Until the handmade knife appeared, most of what the stores had to sell were variations of the Bowie, not considered practical for either camp chores or as an aid to cleaning game; yet many manufacturers kept turning these monsters out and the public kept buying these gleaming hunks of steel because they didn't have much choice, and since this is what the manufacturers were offering, the knife-buying public thought this was what they really should have. Some imaginative souls even cut these monsters down to proper working size, and some even put war surplus bayonets to the grinding wheel. When the benchmade knife first appeared, knife users swiftly saw what the revolution had wrought; smaller blades, practical sheaths, comfortable handles, and the old manufacturers weren't far behind.

Pete Kershaw, a new name in commercial knifemaking, introduced his

(Left to right) A Harold Corby knife with cocobolo and slight palm swell; a full-tang knife by master knifemaker Rod Chappel with intricate, flowing lines; a model by Roger Russell with slightly less radical lines; and a simple hunter with stag by Issacs of Alaska.

line, and a stainless variety was also offered. What all this meant to the knife buyer and user was a fine selection of knives, many crafted of the same materials as the custom knife, at less than half the price charged for the high-priced brand. This is not intended to put down benchmade knives, but to show that custom knife-men introduced more than change with their fancy products. It would be fair to say, and I doubt that many would argue with this evaluation, that a number of well-crafted factory knives can favorably compete with anything turned out by the fancy folk of a few years ago. While the benchmade knife group has slowly turned to collectors who are willing to pay the prices for quality work, the factor-ies, with their great expertise, are filling the void for an honest working knife. Esthetics aside, if the benchmade blade held an edge longer than a factory knife, it was obviously worth the extra money. But we are talking of a half-dozen years ago, when custom knives cost an average of $50, with some even less. Now that the selling price of a benchmade knife has topped $100, with name makers charging $300 to $500, the factory product is still selling for considerably less. The stores are now offering knives with excellent drop-point blades, particularly Gerber's products, with good sheaths and quality steels (even 440-C), and they are excellent bargains for about $40.

For most sportsmen, performance is what counts in a blade, and the per-formance factor in a custom blade has not increased, only the price and decor.

52

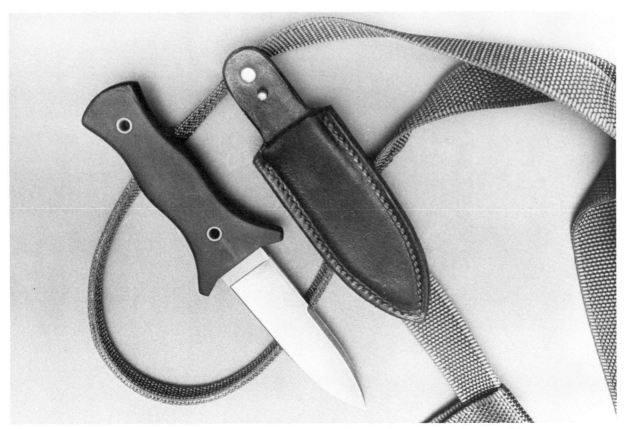

A modern boot knife with sheath, and a knife designed by Blackie Collins. The shoulder rig allows the knife to be worn upside down, and the large pin in the sheath prevents the knife from falling out. The handle is of Lexan, a bulletproof material.

Bob Loveless once said, "All that fancy work on a knife won't make it work any better, it just ups the price." This is not to imply that custom knives aren't any better; they *are* in the fancy field. But when the performance factor is considered—edge holding in use—knives crafted of equal steel, and properly heat-treated, will work equally well.

There are still many new craftsmen who offer fine knives at modest prices, and such men as Clifton Schneck, Gordon Johnson, the Davis brothers, Gray Taylor, and Frank Vought still do some astounding work at fairly modest prices.

Now that the reader has probably learned more about knives and knife-making than he wanted to know, he can eliminate anguished and frustating waits by crafting his own knives.

Once the kit has introduced the craftsmen to knifemaking, he is ready to move on to the next step and craft a knife with hand tools. This will teach the many methods of shaping a blade, working with files, mixing epoxy, and polishing the blade with emery paper—all the skills necessary in making a knife.

5 || KNIFE CONCEPT AND DESIGN

The most important consideration in creating a practical working knife is to understand fully what a good knife really is, what the blade is to be used for, how it will be used, and what type of handle is necessary to drive and guide the blade. Visitors to a quality knife show will view some pretty far-out knives along with more practical designs, but the extreme efforts should be considered a knifemaker's exercise in design and nothing else for the present.

If a small hunting knife, say for birds and small game, is to be made, the blade shouldn't be too long or too thick. There are, indeed, many areas to consider. One of these is blade shape. In other words, does the blade suit the task intended? Have the proper materials been chosen for both blade and handle? Will the finished knife be pleasing both to the eye and to the touch? And when everything is said and done, does the entire package make sense?

The first rule of thumb is never put anything into the design that isn't necessary. By this we don't mean some tasteful decor which will not interfere with the knife in use, but choils that are too large, or bulky quillions, or a blade shape that isn't correct for the task intended.

First, bear in mind that no one knife will handle every chore set to it, and it is useless to even attempt to make an all-around knife. There just isn't any such thing and never will be.

Best of all is some intelligent observation in the field of why a knife does what it does, plus some solid experience on hunting trips observing guides and others experienced in knife use. Obviously, a small blade conceived for eastern hunting won't do on larger game in our western states or north of the border. And a longer blade might be difficult working on grouse or rabbits. The more expert a man becomes with a knife, the less machete-like it will have to be. A smaller knife will be more comfortable to carry all day in the field. And since the trend is toward small blades, about 3 to 3½ inches in length, they can be a lesser nuisance when skinning or dressing out game or working inside the body of bigger animals. Perhaps moderation should be the key word when dreaming up a design for the ideal knife.

There are other wild and woolly gimmicks the beginner should resist. For example, the most useless gadget ever shown was a guthook on a fillet knife, with the maker, a professional, proclaiming the ease of zipping open the belly of a big fish. The whole concept frightened me. Unfortunately, a not too uncommon trap for the eager professional is undertaking a customer's impractical design. The amateur knifeman need not fall into this quagmire, since he has no one to please but himself.

Another good hint is to study the work of the top knifemakers and the men who conceive the most unique knives. One of these craftsmen, a man who comes up with the most innovative ideas year after year, is Blackie Collins of Rock Hill, S.C. In 1972, Collins introduced the Survivor Belt, a double-edged dagger worn as a belt buckle. It was an immediate hit and is still being crafted by the Bowen Knife Company in Georgia. After this success, Collins went on to design an entire line of knives for Smith & Wesson, including a survival knife and a folder. At the 1977 Knifemakers Guild show in Kansas City, Collins came out with the Ninja, a thin, unique boot knife that could be worn in a shoulder rig, on the belt either right or left side or upside down. The trick was a spring steel pin built into the sheath snapping into the knife handle to hold it in place. The handle is injection-molded Lexan which is bulletproof, the blade 440-C, and the entire rig is well conceived. Collins is perhaps the most creative knife designer today, and more important, he follows the project through from blade to handle to sheath.

Another forward-thinking design is that of Larry Hendricks of Mesa, Arizona. Within the confines of the handle on a 4-inch hunter, Hendricks has designed a small scalpel-like caping knife for trophy game. Named the Kangaroo, and patented by Hendricks, the unique feature of the smaller blade might be the ideal answer for the sportsman who must pack his gear into high country. Both blades are made of 440-C and the entire package shows innovative thought on the part of the maker.

One of the most unusual modern knife designs is a folder by Paul Poehlmann, a research and development engineer in the aerospace industry. When the knife was first shown at the Knifemakers Guild show in Texas a few years ago, it quickly became a collector's item, although it was priced in the $300 range. The concept of the knife is unique, since the blade is without a nail nick because one isn't required to open and close the blade. The axial locking mechanism set into the bolster is the outstanding feature of the knife since, quite simply, two buttons are pressed with thumb and forefinger to swing the blade open and closed.

Realizing that it wouldn't be possible to maintain any type of mass production in a one-man shop, Poehlmann selected Gerber to produce the knife, knowing that it was the one commercial cutlery firm that could maintain his own high standards of quality in a mass-produced knife.

These men have made their mark on handcrafted knives, since each has

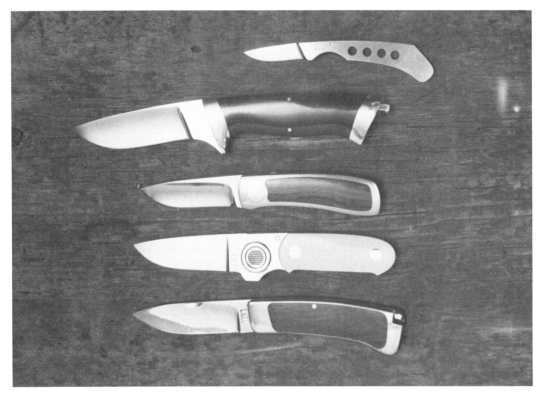

Perhaps the most innovative knives in the long history of knifemaking. (Top to bottom) The Larry Hendricks Kangaroo knife with a small caping blade that slides into the handle; and three folders by Barry Wood, Paul Poehlmann, and Ron Lake, all with unique methods of opening and closing which seem to delight knife collectors.

contributed something new and unique in knife design. They join Barry Wood and Ron Lake in imaginative concepts which prove that something as simple as a knife is constantly undergoing evolution and being steadily improved.

Probably one of the most important considerations for the beginner in knifemaking is to select the steel, then decide on guard and handle materials. While the inexperienced knifemaker may be somewhat confused, he can do no better, as we said earlier, than to select a steel used by his favorite knifeman. In recent years the availability of some excellent stainless alloys have given the lie to the belief that rust-resistant steels won't make a good knife blade. While 154-CM or 440-C may be a bit more difficult to sharpen, that is a small price to pay for a blade that will hold an edge longer at the start.

The thickness of the blank selected is also important, but a matter of personal preference. Some men like a heavy knife and use 1/4-inch stock. While this is eventually ground down, it still leaves a pretty thick spine and makes a fairly hefty knife. Other craftsmen have taken the opposite tack and use 1/8-inch steel, which makes a very light and delicate knife. J. D. Clay, a top professional, crafts his popular Model II Fish & Bird knife of 1/8-inch steel and with a tapered tang; it is a handsome knife for small game and fish. Incidentally, Clay has settled on 440-C exclusively because he feels that it makes a knife that will satisfy the discriminating sportsman and collector. Ted Dowell goes further than that and crafts his Featherweight and Utility knives from 3/32-inch stock, delivering a knife with hardwood handles and metal pins tipping the scales at 2¼ ounces. This is another ideal knife

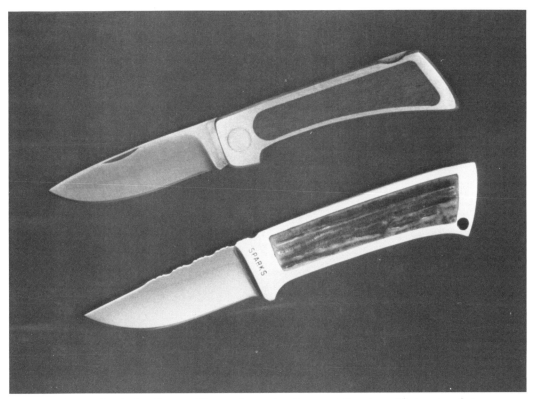

An inter-frame knife by Jimmy Lile and one by Bernard Sparks with insets of stag.

for the backpacker or mountain climber and anyone else who must consider weight.

Master cutler Bob Loveless offers some of his knives in 3/16-inch stock— so it can be seen by the variety of steel thicknesses offered by the various knife-makers that there is some small difference of opinion on stock for the ideal blade. For the novice knifemaker, 3/16-inch stock might be the best, since it won't have to be ground down too much from heavy stock and yet it won't be so thin that too much steel will be removed too quickly on the grinding belts.

On the advice of knifemen Jim Small and George Herron, A-2 should be the choice for the beginner since they feel it is the easiest steel to cut on the band-saw and will present fewer problems during grinding. Added to that is the excellent polish A-2 takes, eliminating any difficulty in that area of knifemaking.

A guard of brass is traditional on most knives and blends with many of the woods or wood Micarta, and it handles nicely. Yet brass is heavy, and a guard and butt cap on a stick-handle knife can add a fair amount of weight. Of course, a tapered tang knife doesn't require a butt cap, and many won't even have a guard in the traditional sense, just a small choil or slight cut in the metal to prevent the hand from sliding down onto the blade.

By all means, if the craftsman considers brass as an attractive addition, he should use it. Many favor nickle silver but find it somewhat difficult to solder. A growing number of knifemakers are leaning toward stainless steel as an ideal guard material. It grinds well, takes a handsome polish, and is fairly impervious to nicks and scratches. Any of these materials may be obtained from the various knifemaker's supply houses.

A cased pair of knives by Jim Nolen. At the top is a small bird and trout model with a walnut burl handle, and at the bottom is a matching gut-hook skinner.

Handle materials can be confusing, but as Jim Small says, "Micarta makes the best working knife handle, bar none." It is also a material used by practically every professional knifemaker. It grinds well, takes an excellent polish, and is hard and tough. Micarta is also impervious to any of the hazards of the outdoors— and that includes a quick fall into a roaring campfire. It will resist rain, won't warp, doesn't change shape, and won't be affected by the heat and humidity of a rain forest or the cold climes of some freezing mountain peak. It is, quite simply, the best handle material for a working knife.

What about fiber liners for a full-tang knife or as spacers for a stick-handle knife? They may be used if desired if the maker feels they will add to the knife. Obviously, spacers on a stick-handle knife have a couple of reasons for being. They add to the beauty of the handle and permit the craftsman to add or remove spacers for a proper fit. The spacer material may be purchased in sheets or even in small precut squares at quite reasonable prices.

With a decision on materials made, what type or style of knife should be selected for the first effort? With the trend toward smaller blades, anything between three and four inches should be efficient in use and easy to handle. There is little doubt that the drop-point leads in popularity, and many sportsmen feel it makes the task of working on game easier. As with all things in knifemaking, there is some difference of opinion as to the easiest knife for the beginner to make. Some expert knifemen vote for the stick-handle, feeling that it is much easier to drill a hole for the tang, pour in some epoxy, and shape the handle for a finished knife. Others feel that shaping a full-tang knife is not too difficult, and once the slabs are set with epoxy and pins, it is much easier to do everything together. Since both methods are shown, the reader will have to decide which may be best for him.

As to style of knife to be crafted, a careful perusal of the photographs in this book should inspire the beginner and perhaps get his creative juices running full tilt.

The type of grind should also be given consideration. There are two basic styles found on modern blades: hollow and flat. We'll eliminate such intricate work as Rod Chappel's boot knife, which has hollow grinds on the two top sections and a convex grind on the bottom. Chappel is a masterful grinder, perhaps one of the best in the business, but his skills are beyond the ability of most beginners. Of course, much depends on the type of equipment available to the beginner and his skill with machines.

For example, Lloyd Hale has a 6- by 48-inch horizontal flat grinder to flatten and true his bar stock. While bars of steel look flat, most pieces have as many curves as a belly dancer and must be ground true if future trouble is to be eliminated.

The Bader, Square Wheel, or Burr-King grinders are required for hollow grinding, although with the various platen attachments, some smaller knife blades may be flat-ground on these machines. A newer and less costly piece of equipment was recently introduced called the Speed-Cut belt grinder-buffer. It has many interesting features and heavy-duty construction. Price as of this writing is $164.95, and it may be used on motors from 1/2 to 1 horsepower. This is considerably less than other grinders, which sell customarily for between $500 and $1,000 and could well be the ideal tool for the part-time craftsman who doesn't want to make a big investment in equipment. Metal-cutting bandsaws can cost around $300, and a hefty drill press can add another couple of hundred dollars to your costs.

Many knifemakers, including George Herron, Michael Collins, and Jim Small, use the Sears flat grinder to attain their magnificent flat-ground blades; this grinder costs about $300.

George Herron feels that the amateur knifemaker can get along with one good grinder, a drill press, and a fairly good amount of assorted files, clamps, and other hand tools. Even a buffing wheel may be used on the drill press for polishing and the grinder for profiling the blade. These, then, are the basic tools needed to make a knife.

As for supplies, the part-time craftsman does not have to purchase them in huge quantities. He can order material for one knife or a dozen.

Again, a word of caution: regardless of the type of knife to be made, work slowly and have patience; keep foremost in your mind that every small step, if done with care, will add to the overall appearance of the finished knife.

6

SAFETY IN THE SHOP

Before undertaking any work either in the workshop or on the kitchen table, there are some areas of safety that should be brought to the attention of the beginner.

In spite of the casual attitude of experienced knifemen toward their craft, all, without exception, will eventually bring up a number of hazards to be found working with wood or steel.

Machines in knifemaking shops run at exceptionally high speeds and can be extremely hazardous to both the experienced knifemaker and the new craftsman. Take a bandsaw, for example. Throughout this book the reader will note that many knifemakers use a push stick or rod when their fingers get too close to the saw blade or grinder. Although there are varying opinions as to the most dangerous task in knifemaking, many men rate the bandsaw and the buffing wheel as the top hazards. One mistake, one bit of careless attention to the job at hand, and suddenly a fingertip is gone.

Eyes should also be protected, and a face shield or safety goggles should be worn when doing even the most simple task. In fact, when it comes to the belt grinder, some craftsmen opt for the full-face shield, which gives better protection. Steel is dangerous, and flying chips can become deeply embedded in the eyeball. A good eye doctor can usually remove steel with a magnet, but brass and aluminum are also used and these splinters can present serious problems. The eyes should always be protected. The fun and satisfaction of making a knife cannot be traded off against the loss of an eye.

Probably the greatest hazards result from grinding or polishing. Micartas, steel, brass, and some of the woods offer many dangers. Cocobolo, one of the most beautiful of the exotic woods used for knife handles, can cause a skin rash, fever, or coughing fits in some people. Mother-of-pearl, abalone, or various shells

Good shop practice demonstrated by George Herron, using mask, safety glasses, and gloves during rough grinding.

George Herron uses a push rod as a protection for his fingers.

are like glass and cannot be absorbed by the lungs. An added danger with grinding shell material is that it gives off a deadly cyanide gas while being ground and polished.

Everything that doesn't fall to the floor may be sucked into the lungs, and while the results may not show up immediately, the long-range prospects aren't good. Face masks and respirators can be a help and should even be worn in a well-ventilated shop.

A few years ago when Ted Dowell went for his yearly physical, X-rays showed a tiny spot on one lung. Dowell frankly admits it scared him, but fortunately, further tests proved negative—the cause was Micarta dust. Although Dowell had always worn a small surgical mask, he quickly went to double-snout, double-filter respirator, and the problem cleared up.

Even buffing compounds of abrasive particles are suspended in the air, and if it can be smelled it certainly can be inhaled. Something as innocent and simple as soldering should be approached with a certain amount of caution. Solders and fluxes frequently have poisonous substances in their base, and if the instructions say to work in a well-ventilated area, do so. Drilling holes with a drill press? Heck, nothing to it. Well, there really is, and that's another danger. Clamp everything tight so that the work won't be yanked out, and don't get careless with those steel chips. Use a small brush to clear the work area. Those curly little pieces of steel cut like razors.

Perhaps most greatly feared by knifemen are buffing wheels, because the

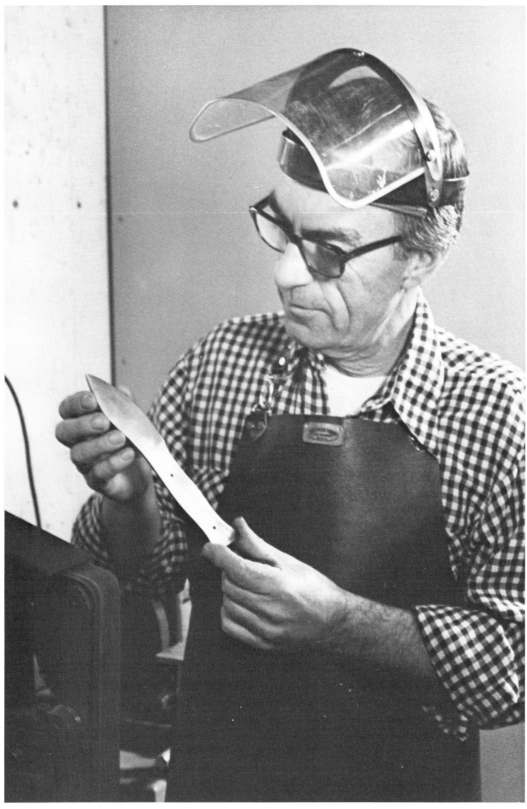

Jack Barnett with a full-face shield and a leather apron. The mask is worn during grinding.

Bill Moran uses long tongs to draw a Damascus blade in oil. Heavy gloves, apron, and safety glasses protect him during the operation.

64

soft material can grab a knife and toss it into the maker's foot or thigh. Most professional knifemakers admit to having a healthy respect for their machines, and it is a rare craftsman who has not had a serious accident sometime in his career.

Someone is sure to ask why, if there are so many dangers to the hands, do knifemakers not wear heavy gloves? The reason is that the knifemaker must retain the sensitivity in his fingers. When the steel becomes hot, it must be dunked into a bucket of water. If it isn't, the steel will burn as well as fingers.

Now that the beginner has probably been thoroughly frightened, let us temper the bad news with the good. As we said earlier, patience is the one prime requisite in knifemaking. If there is no attempt to hurry or speed up work, there will be less chance of accidents. Pay strict attention to what is going on and don't start daydreaming while profiling a blade or grinding a guard.

Perhaps most of all, a proper frame of mind is basic to working on knives with high-speed machines. Distressed or upset, an argument with someone, or concern about business—then forget it. Do anything, but stay out of the shop during those low periods. Care and caution will ensure greater success with the first venture in knifemaking, and the fewer accidents in the beginning, the greater the confidence later.

7

JACK BARNETT: THE STICK-HANDLE KNIFE AND THE BOOT KNIFE

Among the many knifemakers I've met over the past half-dozen years, none has impressed me more than a former law-enforcement officer by the name of Jack Barnett. Barnett has seen duty with the Alaska State Police and the Iowa Bureau of Criminal Investigation and now lives quietly in Littleton, Colorado, with a lovely wife and a couple of beagles. Barnett is one of the few knifemakers I know who likes to maintain a low profile; yet his talents as a double-threat craftsman—knife-maker and skilled leatherworker—demand inclusion in this book.

Barnett puts in many ten-hour days in a well-equipped shop in the basement of his home crafting top-quality knives. In a small adjacent area is a first-class leather shop sufficient to turn out anything from saddles to knife sheaths, although Barnett draws the line at anything larger, admitting he just doesn't have time for elaborate items. The first knives and sheaths he made were during a turn in the navy in the South Pacific with materials liberated from the sail locker, and since that time Barnett has improved his skills tremendously. Equally at home with steel or leather, Barnett says: "I'd be hard pressed to choose between making knives or working with leather since I enjoy both."

Unlike many knifemen, Barnett does not offer a wide-ranging variety of styles, keeping to five or six models at most. These include a couple of hunting models, a trim-looking trout and bird model that would allow a surgeon to remove an appendix in an emergency, a sleek boot knife, and on occasion, a matched bowie and tomahawk set. Jack does not do folders, having no interest in them. As far as the collector's race is concerned, he said, "I want to do practical, sensible, sportsman's knives. Make them superbly well and sell them for honest prices." That he has accomplished this is shown by the backlog of orders hanging in his shop from around the country and a host of foreign lands.

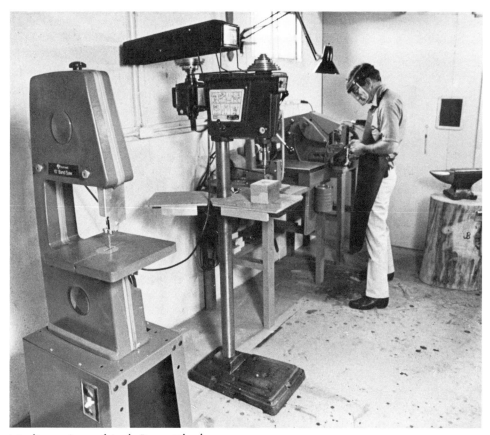

Medium view of Jack Barnett's shop.

Like most professional knifemen, Barnett has his own views on steel. His first preference is D-2. At the same time, he admits that carbon tool steels aren't as sophisticated as the stainless varieties. For the amateur knifemaker, however, Barnett feels that the carbon steels might be a better choice for a number of reasons: O-1 will grind nicely and can be heat-treated with less concern than the stainless 440-C or 154-CM. Jack would encourage any new craftsman, making his first few knives, to also use a commercial heat-treating firm. Although he has done his own heat-treating in the past, Barnett feels that time can best be devoted to making knives rather than in the involved process of heat-treating your own blades. Added to that is the initial investment for expensive furnaces when a blade may be commercially heat-treated for an average price of about $10.

Barnett's other choices for steels, aside from O-1, a good beginner's steel, are A-2 and perhaps the stainless or rust-resistant 440-C. Barnett also cautions us not to have the blade heat-treated too hard. Follow the advice of the heat-treater since the experts know the predetermined hardness for each type of steel.

Once the amateur craftsman has learned to grind and polish well, and do everything else to make a good knife, he can go on to other steels, such as 440-C or 154-CM. Fortunately, knifemaking has become sufficiently popular to allow the aspiring knifemaker to order a few blanks of different steels to try them out.

As to his own skills, Barnett says, "I'm one of the fellows who fell off the turnip truck years ago and just started making knives. I don't want to be the best knifemaker in the world nor do I intend to try." His own modesty is directly opposite his reputation as a craftsman, and most of Barnett's admirers tend to take his self-effacement with a grain of salt. As Joe Davis of Knife World, a successful knife shop in neighboring Englewood, Colorado, says, "Any guy with eighteen months of orders can't be all bad." Barnett readily admits that knifemaking is infectious and even carries over to his collecting the work of other makers. As to making knives: "First the knife must satisfy me, and then it must satisfy the customer."

As to styles, Barnett regards the modern drop-point as perhaps the most useful and functional type of blade for the modern hunter. Short blades are also his favorite, although years ago, when he was living in Alaska, longer blades were popular. Large bowies are pretty as decoration in a den but have little use in the field.

Clean lines are important to a knife, and it is obvious from the models offered that Barnett has followed his own advice. "While the blade must be good-looking, its design must also be functional to its intended use."

The greatest amount of effort in the design of a knife is in the handle. A cutting blade is the working part of the knife, but the handle is the portion that marries it to the individual using that tool and gives control of the cutting edge. The handle is an extremely important part of any knife, and Barnett would encourage any amateur to give much thought to the use of the knife and the design and eventual shape of the handle before he even begins work.

Unorthodox in his techniques, Barnett, for example, prefers to buff his blades on the drill press. Using a large buffing wheel fastened to the chuck, Barnett buffs his blades in a vertical position. He claims he cannot see the blade too well using the horizontal method, and should the soft buffing cloth grab the blade, it will be thrown away from him. He probably does more hand work on both blade and handle than many other makers. Where most will use the sanding belt for complete forming of the handle, Barnett will just rough out and then hand sand, using various grits of paper. The same with polishing blades: after shaping, he will begin to polish, using successively finer grits to obtain a fine finish. All this takes time, but more important to Barnett, it gives him the satisfaction of doing it his own way and certainly adds more to a handmade knife.

Making the Stick-Handle Knife

In making a knife, the first thing is to select the blade style, make a template, and choose the steel. The stick-handle knife shown was made of 440-C and is basically a simple knife to craft.

It has a brass guard but no butt cap. The wood for the handle is manzanita, an ironwood from the high country of Mexico, with natural resin finish. It is buffed on completion.

The outline of the blade is scribed onto the steel. Barnett does very little sawing of the steel, and most of the profile is done with a 50-grit belt. Naturally, a bucket of water must be kept nearby in which to keep dipping the steel so it won't be burned.

After profiling, it is placed against the flat platen on the Square-Wheel grinder to flatten the stock should it not be precision-ground. The choil is put in

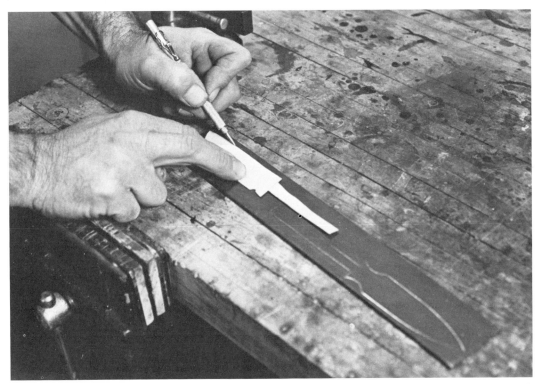

Template used to mark out both boot knife and stick-handle knife on one piece of steel.

Barnett profiles the blade on the grinder. Note the profile line and the amount of metal to be removed.

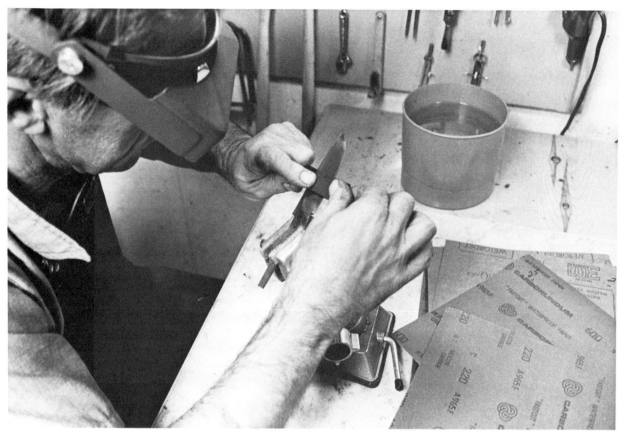

After the excess metal is removed and the blade ground to shape, Barnett places the knife in a vise and proceeds to shape it by hand, using various grades of emery paper. It is important to change the direction of sanding with each change of paper.

by drilling a hole and then grinding out on the edge of the belt. Next the blade is flat-ground. This is done by scribing two lines down the cutting edge of the blade to give a guide. This is done on an 80-grit belt. Grind down to the cutting edge at a 45° bevel. It is sometimes helpful to use a template that may be used over again as a guide for other blades of the same type. Even the grind lines may be placed on the template. From the 80-grit, move on to a 100-grit belt, then finish with the 220-grit. After the blade has been ground, but without a cutting edge, the blade is hand-sanded. Start with a 220-grit either wet or dry, then 320, 400, and 600. During the hand-sanding the direction of the sanding stroke is alternated with each change of paper. Once this is done, the maker's name may be stamped on the ricasso. The next step is to buff on the drill press. Actually, by hand-sanding to such a fine finish, too much buffing is not required.

Two compounds are used for the first buffing, Brownell's 555 and Green Chrome rouge, which is used last. Barnett's technique is to use a stitched wheel and when using the final fine compound, three rows of stitching are cut off to make a sloppy buffing wheel. Barnett feels that this gives a better polish.

At this stage the blade is polished but not sharpened. The thumb serration on the back of the blade is done with a mill file and is likened to checkering on a gun. It will give a solid purchase for the thumb when the knife is used. Now the blade is ready for heat-treating. As a suggestion, Barnett advises drilling a small

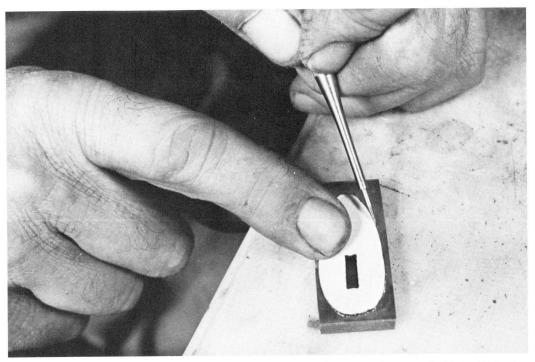

A template is used to mark out the guard on a piece of brass stock 1/4 inch thick, 1½ inches long, and 3/4 inch wide.

hole near the top of the tang. This will allow the heat-treater to hang the blade when it is in the chamber and this is helpful in avoiding warpage. Although the blade has been mirror-polished, it will be returned from the heat-treatment with a smoky gray finish that is easily buffed off.

Although many makers don't send their blades off with a high polish, Barnett does fancy file work on many of his blades and finds it necessary to bring the blade to a high polish before having the blade heat-treated.

Once the smoky surface has been buffed, the brass guard is put on. This is 1/4-inch bar stock and two holes are scribed and drilled in the guard, and the excess brass is sawed out with a small jeweler's saw to a slightly smaller size than the tang. The final tight fit is filed out using needle files. By trial and error a final fit is achieved. A proper fit is important because a guard with too large a hole requires too much solder, and the craftsman is apt to end up with a bad-looking solder joint. When the fit is correct and sits over the shoulders snugly, the guard is now ready for silver solder. Barnett uses a low-melting silver solder and sets the blade in a vise to hold it in place. When the guard is set onto the tang, the silver solder is done from the top. Jack feels there is no excuse for any solder to be slobbered around the guard. He uses a small steel ruler to remove any excess material, then takes a piece of well-worn 600-grit paper and hand-sands the top of the guard and then buffs lightly. This will make a good-looking joint and is important in a hand-made knife. Next the spacer material is set on, and then the edges of the tang are checkered with a file to allow more bite for the epoxy. An oblong hole is drilled in the handle material to receive the tang. The fit must be perfect; it cannot be angled and must be in correct proportions to the guard. Otherwise, an epoxy joint will show, and this indicates some carelessness on the part of the maker. With a

71

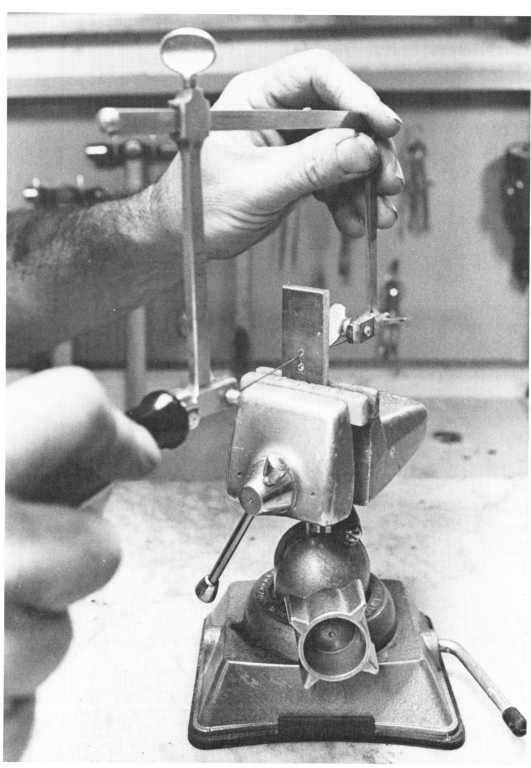

After drilling two holes with the drill press, a saw blade is passed through the holes and the marked-off center section is sawed out.

72

Files are used to obtain a proper, tight fit for the tang.

The knife tang is held by a clamp and the guard soldered on.

Crosshatching is placed atop the blade for thumb purchase when using the knife.

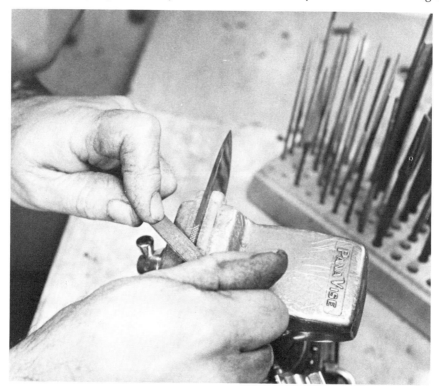

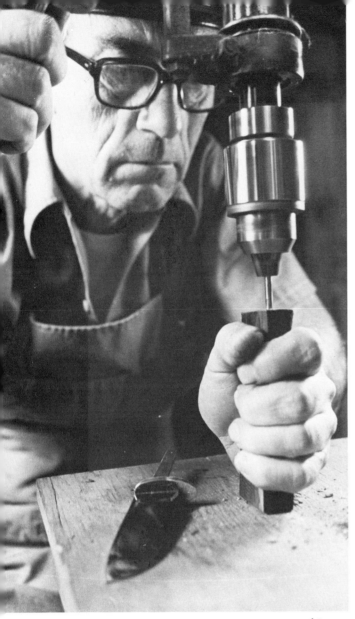

A block of manzanita wood is cut and drilled for the tang to pass through.

With spacers already on, the tang is set into the wood block and checked for fit.

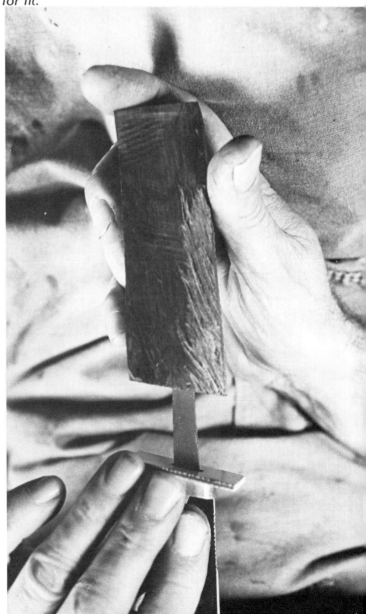

Epoxy is poured into the tang hole in the handle block and coated on both sides of the spacers and around the tang.

little practice and careful attention, this can be made to fit so there isn't even a hairline showing.

Both sides of the spacers are covered with epoxy, the tang is also covered, and epoxy fills the hole in the handle. To get a tight fit, the tip of the blade is pushed into a small block of wood and then fastened with a pipe clamp and turned up with a slight amount of pressure. Barnett doesn't use quick-drying epoxy and allows it to set at least 24 hours.

The next morning the knife is solidly affixed to the spacers and handle and the next step is to shape the handle. The belt-sander is used with a 100-grit belt to shape the guard first. Since low-melting solder was used, it will begin to melt at 400°F, so the knife must constantly be dipped in water as with profiling or blade shaping.

The rough shaping of the handle may be done on the bandsaw, but rough grinding is done on the belt sander. Jack admits to being a little old-fashioned, but he likes to shape his handles by hand. He tapes the blade to protect it and sets it in a vise. Using a wood rasp first, he then moves on to the various grits of paper for a final finish. Oddly enough, Barnett washes the entire knife in Palmolive liquid soap to remove all the grit, dust, and buffing compounds. The only thing left is to inspect the knife and see if you made one to your satisfaction. "If you did," says Barnett, "then that's the time to stop knifemaking since you've made the perfect knife."

Now to sharpening. Jack sharpens a knife on a 1- by 24-inch belt sander using a 220-grit belt. Remember that this is actually a little bit of grinding since

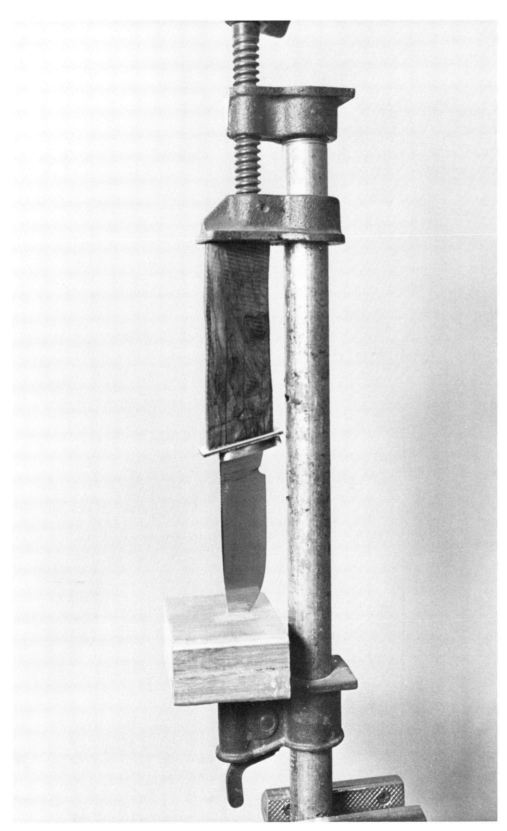

With the point pressed into a block of wood, a pipe clamp is used to tighten with sufficient downward pressure, and the handle is allowed to set overnight.

When everything is completely dry, a bandsaw is used to cut excess wood off the handle.

Rough-sanding the handle to shape.

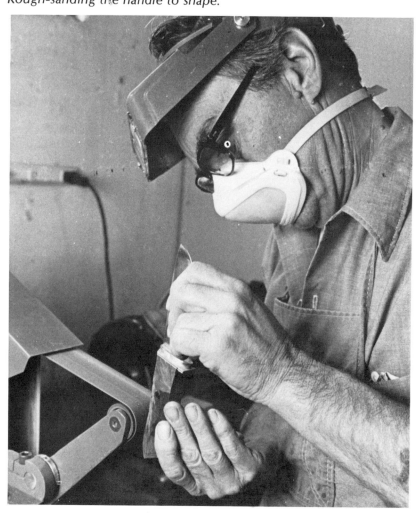

Barnett begins to use emery paper to complete shaping of the handle. Begin with a 60 grit and finish with 600 grit.

Final buffing on the vertical drill press, using the buffing wheel and green rouge compound.

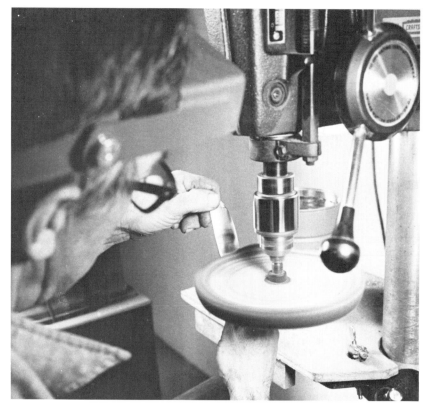

Same vertical buffing technique as was used to buff the blade.

Fine sanding belt used for placing an edge on a knife. This is the final step in making a knife.

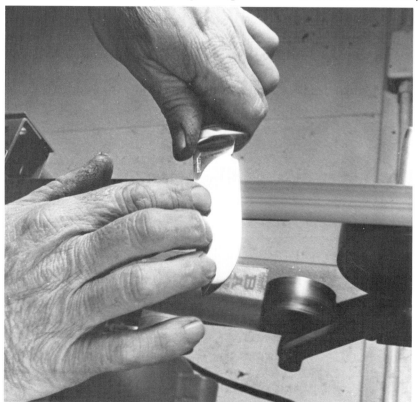

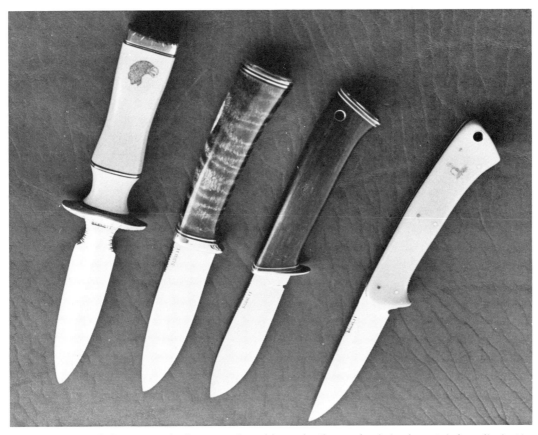

Four of Barnett's knives with the completed boot knife on the left, the stick-handle knife, a small drop-point knife, and a tapered-tang trout knife with an ivory Micarta handle.

there is still a very small flat surface along the edge of the blade that has never been ground to a bevel. Once the proper edge has been put on, Jack moves to the buffer, and incidentally, this is the only time he uses the buffer. A hard felt wheel is attached and the sharpened edge is buffed. Again water is used for dipping the blade since the buffing wheel generates tremendous heat and the blade must be kept cool. Barnett is one of the many knifemakers who stresses the hazard of buffing, saying, "This is one of the most dangerous parts of knifemaking and since the wheel turns downward, stand slightly sideways to the wheel." Incidentally, don't buff the thumb serrations atop the blade since the buffer will grind them down, dull the sharpened edges, and defeat the purpose of their use.

Making the Boot Knife

Well, the stick-handle knife is now complete. It probably wasn't as easy as you expected or quite as difficult as you imagined. Sure there were little problems, but these will be overcome when making the next knife. The boot knife is going to be a bit more difficult. On a scale of one to ten the boot knife might be an eight, since it has four sides that must be ground equal. Barnett likens it to grinding four knives. The many parts of the handle will offer some obstacles, but patience and perseverance will produce an excellent boot knife.

The boot knife blade is made of 440-C steel with white Micarta handle material. Nickle silver is used for the guard and butt cap as well as spacers between black fiber material in three different places on the handle. Decorative file work is executed on the guard, around the throat or double choils, and butt cap. Barnett usually places a small scrimshawed eagle head on the handle for added decor.

The knife is double-edged, and even Barnett admits it isn't the easiest knife for him to make. Although it is flat-ground, both sides must be absolutely symmetrical and meet in a perfect center line running exactly to the point. This must be done on both sides of the blade.

As with the stick-handle hunting knife, a template must be made and scribed onto the steel. Particular attention must be paid to the length of the tang, since it will have a threaded butt cap to screw onto the end of the tang. This will take up tightly and hold the various parts of the handle in position. Incidentally, this handle, counting the two larger white Micarta parts, including spacers and butt, has twelve pieces, which makes it slightly more complicated than either a regular stick- or tapered-tang handle.

As with the first knife, profile grinding is done on the Square Wheel grinder using an 80-grit belt. The shoulders of the guard must be perfectly square to the center line of the blade. If this isn't done, the double guard will cant at an angle and be noticeable when the knife is completed.

Once the blade has been rough-profiled, both choils opposite the ricasso are ground out with the 80-grit belt. A final choil grind may be done with a drum-sander on the drill press, but again, both choils must be exact and match perfectly. Otherwise, the knife will appear out of balance when assembled. Then the cutting edge of the blade is scribed with two lines, leaving a very fine line 1/32-inch wide along both edges. Next a center line is scribed on the flat of the blade down the center, and this should be done with dividers to ensure precise marking.

Begin flat-grinding the sides of the blade and remember that this requires four grinds that must match perfectly. Again, begin with a 100-grit belt and keep the bevel 45°.

Stay in that bevel and start working it back toward the center line. The ricassos may present some problems since they are done at the same time. In grinding, as a reminder, an 80 grit is used for the profile, a 100 grit for the beginning grind, and as the work progresses, change to a 220 belt and progress to successively finer grits as with the previous knife. In grinding the ricasso area, Barnett sometimes uses the platen on the square wheel, saying: "It makes no difference to me what position I'm in; sometimes I'm almost standing on my head, but it's the final result that counts."

Assuming that a double-edged knife has been ground to satisfaction, proceed to hand-sanding the blade using a wet-grit paper. Start with 220, next 320, 400, and 600, and remember to change the stroke direction with each different grit. Barnett suggests using a small block of steel or Micarta as a backing for the paper to give a perfectly flat surface for sanding.

Once the blade has been hand-sanded down through the series of grits, it is placed on the anvil for hand-stamping the maker's name and buffing on the vertical buffer with the same compounds as before.

The tang is threaded using the proper diameter for the thread to be used. The file work is now done on the choils using three files: a small 1/8-inch round file, a needle file, and a micro file, which is the size of a small needle. The patterns

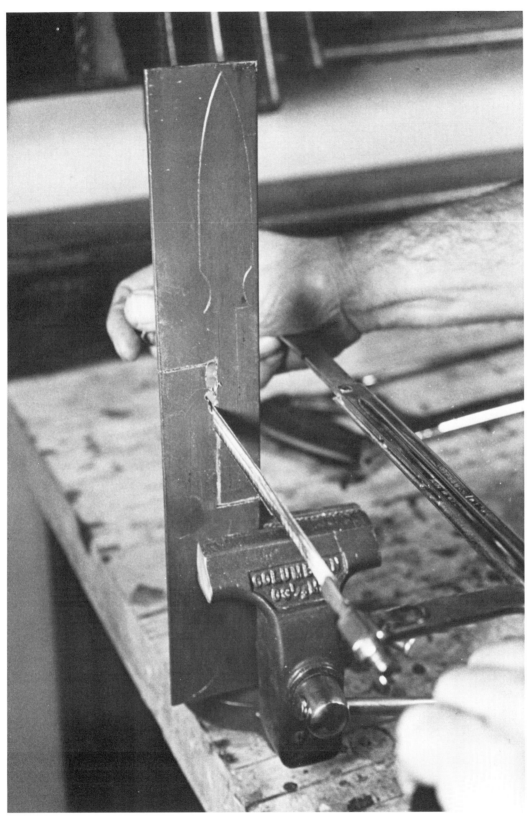

Hacksaw used to cut out the blade from the steel blank.

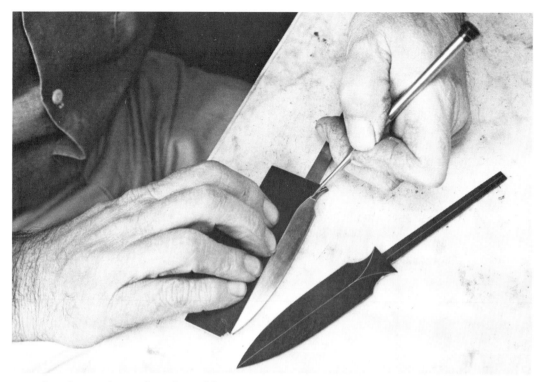

Template for outlining bevels and lines.

A push rod is used for pushing the sawed blank flat against the square wheel grinder to flatten the blank true.

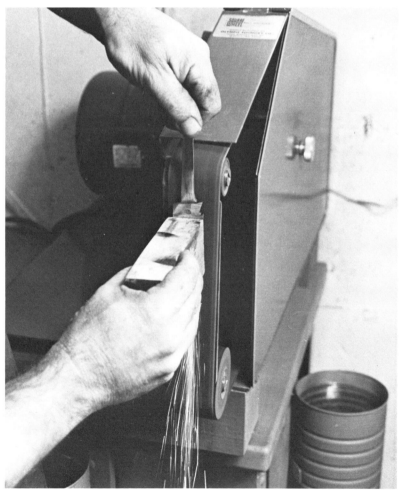

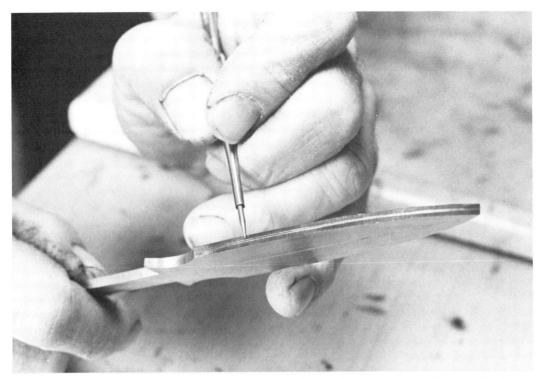

The edge lines scribed along the edge of the blank. This is where control in grinding is evident, because the object is to have perfect symmetry of edge.

Close-up of the grind on one side of the blade. Barnett likens this to making four knives, because four sides must be ground perfectly and meet in a perfectly straight line in the center of the blade on both sides. Start with a 60-grit belt, then progress to finer grits. Each successive grit must remove scratches caused by the previous belt.

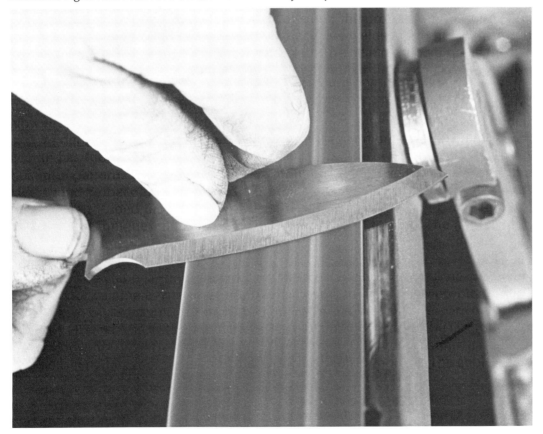

Squaring up the shoulders so that the guard fits properly.

The file work is placed in before heat-treating. This is the way a blade looks after heat-treating: it has a gray, scaly appearance that is easily removed.

for the file work are laid out on the steel, and this work must be done before heat-treating; otherwise, the steel will be too hard. Once the blade is returned from the heat-treater, the smoky finish is again buffed off and it is ready for the guard and handle to be put on.

As with the previous guard, a 1/4-inch piece of nickle silver is cut out, holes scribed, and drilled. The guard may be rough-shaped on the grinder either before or after it is soldered on the blade. Most knifemakers don't wear gloves, in order to feel the heat of the blade and know when to dip it in the water. Barnett says that extreme caution must be used around the sander since it can chew flesh fast and cause some very nasty wounds.

After the guard is soldered, the same method is used as in the stick-handle knife. The Micarta is laid out for the transfer of the tang by pencil, and an oblong hole is drilled in the Micarta. Two small holes are better than one large hole, since it can be drilled and filed for a better fit. From the top another hole is drilled to match the bottom hole. The piece of Micarta is now sawed, and a reference to the illustrations will help at this point. All cuts must be square. All spacers are cut to rough size, and when everything is ready it rather resembles pieces of a jigsaw puzzle.

The butt cap can be a little tricky, so follow directions closely. To prepare the butt cap for the threaded tang, a piece of nickle silver is cut that will grind down to the proper size. Another piece of nickle silver bar stock is cut 1/4 inch long and 3/8 inch square. This is hard-silver-soldered and will bond at 1200°F; this is known as a form of brazing and will retain the butt cap on the knife. A center punch is made and a hole drilled and threaded that will match those on the tang. When this is done, assemble the entire handle *without epoxy* to make certain that everything fits properly.

To obtain the black epoxy that will be used, Brownell's Black epoxy compound is mixed with the clear epoxy to darken it. All parts are covered with the epoxy: both sides of the spacers; the top of the guard; tang, including the threads; and inside the center holes in both pieces of white Micarta that will form the handle. Once all pieces are put on, the butt cap is screwed on and tightened. It must be tight enough to force epoxy out between all the various pieces and give a tight enough fit that no epoxy will show once it is dry and the handle ground down. Don't be concerned when the epoxy starts to ooze out and run, since it will all be ground off eventually. The only precaution the craftsman might take is to tape the blade, since hardened epoxy isn't the easiest thing to remove. Now the knife is clamped as before and allowed to harden for 24 hours.

Once dry, the handle is squared either with the flat platen on the grinder or a rasp. With all traces of epoxy removed, the center line of the blade is marked on to the handle right up to the butt. Begin shaping on the grinder using an 80- or 100-grit belt for the coarse, rough grinding. Then use a wood file, rasp, and finally emery paper, working the handle down to the point when all four sides are even and blend with the knife. Now the handle is again worked down with a 180, 220, 320, 400, and 600 grit when the last vestiges of hand-sanding are removed.

The concave grind atop the butt cap is done on the small wheel grinder. The file work on both the double quillion guard and butt cap is laid out and done with a 3-inch square file, a 1/8-inch round file, and a micro needle file. The buffing is done with the same compounds as were used on the previous knife. A small

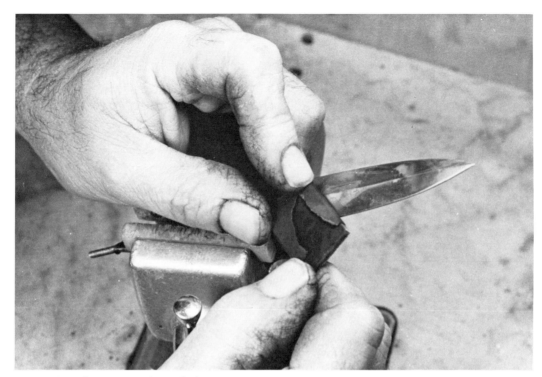

Removing the gray scale with fine emery paper.

Centering the solder marker for the butt cap on a piece of nickle silver.

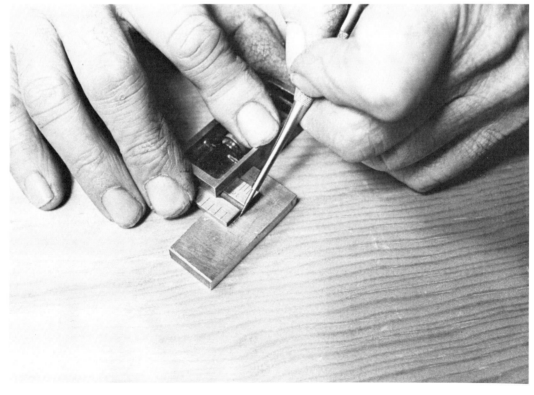

A piece of nickle silver bar stock is 1/4 inch in length and 3/8 inch square. This is hard-silver-soldered or brazed at 1,200°F, then the upright bar is tapped for the proper thread to take up the end of the tang.

With the bar held firmly in a vise, a hole is threaded that will screw onto the now-threaded tang.

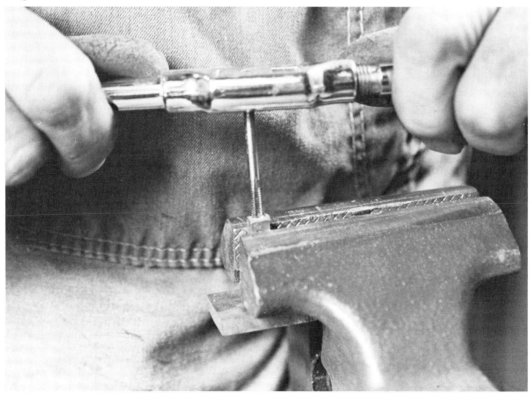

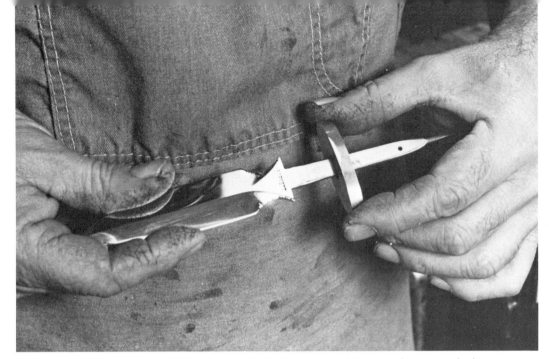

A piece of nickle silver is cut and tried on the tang for fit. Note the extended tang.

Fit snugly against the shoulders, the guard is silver-soldered. Note the filed edges of the tang, which will help in giving the epoxy an area to bite onto.

A small steel ruler is used to remove excess solder. If necessary, Barnett will go to a small-bladed, very sharp knife. Then buffing and polishing will give a smooth finish.

Layout showing how the pieces are set together.

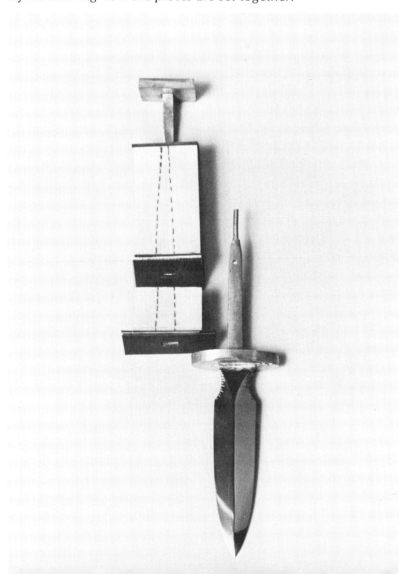

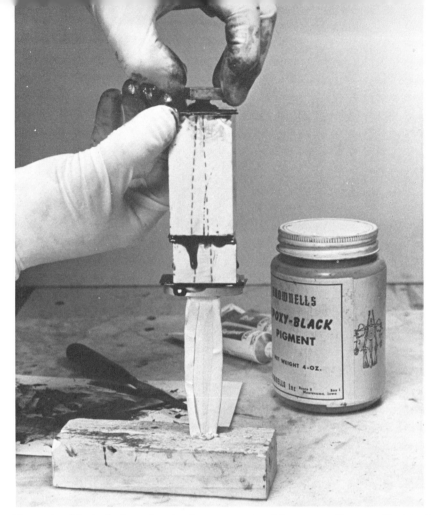

Tape the blade before beginning to work with epoxy. Brownell's black pigment is mixed with clear epoxy and smeared over both sides of the spacers, inside the tang holes, and into the threaded area. The butt cap is threaded down tightly enough to begin to force the epoxy out. Do not be concerned if epoxy dries on the handles, because it will all come off when shaping begins.

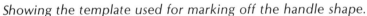

Showing the template used for marking off the handle shape.

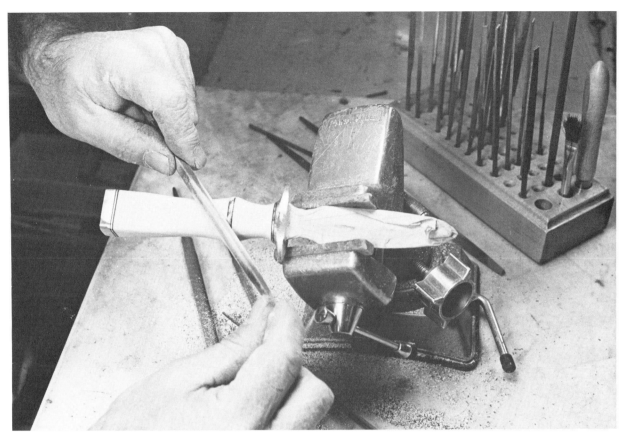

Barnett prefers to shape his handles with various files. Note the blade set in the vise between two pieces of wood.

As the handle begins to take shape, change to finer grits of emery paper.

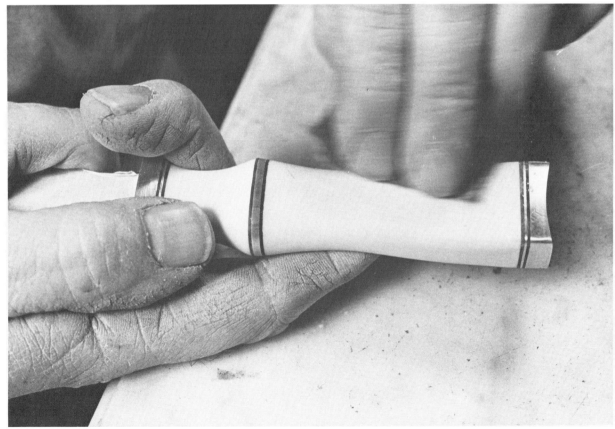

Small files are used for the fancy work around the guard and butt cap. Once this work is complete, a final buffing is done.

Jack Barnett's trademark is a small, scrimshawed eagle head.

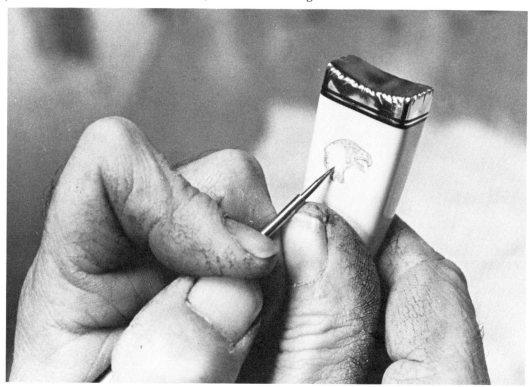

eagle head is scrimshawed and black India ink used to fill the tiny lines. The knife is now complete.

The machines used by Jack Barnett are a flat platen sander, a square wheel grinder, a 1- by 24-inch belt sander, drill press, bandsaw for cutting handle materials, the buffer with a medium-hard felt wheel, and Green Chrome rouge to buff the sharpened edge of the knife. "These are the methods that work for me. They suit me and may be helpful for other craftsmen."

Jack's final word to anyone making knives is: "Don't get in a hurry because it is an entirely new area for any craftsman who hasn't worked with steel. There will be mistakes and first-time efforts will often be disappointing. Keep in mind that nobody ever makes a perfect knife the first time out."

8

GEORGE HERRON: THE FOLDER AND THE TAPERED-TANG HUNTING KNIFE

In the past few years folding knives have attracted the attention of many fine crafts-men. As with straight-bladed knives, there are those who have made exceptionally attractive folders with fancy engraving, ornate handles, and intricate file work on various parts of the metal. Many of these fine folders have been crafted for the sportsman who wanted a small, practical knife to carry in his pocket on trips into the field. Others have gone the collector route with expensive materials and highly ornate blades. One man who is particularly suited to crafting fancy knives is Henry Frank of Whitefish, Montana, who is also one of the finest engravers in the country. The prices of his knives reflect his skill at the top of the ladder, and the majority of his labors end up in collections.

If Henry Frank is sitting on the top rung of skills, this is not to imply that other craftsmen are of lesser talent. Bob Ogg comes to mind as one who makes a practical, sensible folding knife that may be had for comfortably less than $100. Ogg's knives are plain with no locking back, since he uses exceptionally strong springs and his folders will do the job for a man who wants a working knife. Unusual and unique are the folders of Barry Wood and Paul Poehlmann and their cost is commensurate with their craftsmanship and design.

Folding knives are unusual since they will occasionally run higher in price than the regular hunting knife. The reason is easily explained: more parts, greater effort in construction, and longer hours to make a folder. Some craftsmen even specialize in folders to the exclusion of all other types of knives. Paul Fox is a new maker who does exceptionally fine work at modest prices, and Wayne Goddard has been specializing in folders almost since he began making knives a dozen years ago.

Why the big interest in folders? Well, some craftsmen consider it a challenge to their skills, and to be perfectly honest about it, quite a few collectors began to demand folders from their favorite knifemaker.

Among those who picked up the gauntlet is George Herron, regarded as one of the most competent and respected knifemakers in the profession. His work, simple and precise, yet artful in execution and in attention to detail, particularly with folders, is impressive indeed. Herron is one of the few craftsmen who mirror-polishes the liners of a folder, and that is a part of a knife seldom inspected.

Herron, in his mid-forties, has been making knives for about ten years, half of those years as a full-time knifemaker. His previous work as a machinist with the Savannah River Plant of the Atomic Energy Commission gave him excellent training, with intricate equipment, milling and crafting small parts, which carried over into a solid background for the many skills required in crafting knives. About five years ago, taking a twenty-year pension, Herron set up a fully equipped shop in a new addition to his home in Aiken, South Carolina, and began making knives full-time. Now, with a waiting list of customers for the next two years, Herron obviously makes what his clients want. A careful precise worker, Herron reckons he turns out about 175 to 200 knives a year, with folders running about 20 percent of the total. In spite of his popularity Herron still believes in making a modestly priced working knife. The Little Dude, a small tapered-tang sheath knife, is simple yet completely utilitarian. It has a cutting edge of 2¾ inches and a graceful drop-point. This is one of the most popular knives in Herron's line and when Nelson Bryant, the outdoor columnist of the *New York Times*, saw one, he quickly placed an order. The price? A modest $60. And that's the knife we'll be making in this chapter.

Perhaps Herron's folders have captured the greatest interest among knife fanciers. The larger model has a blade 2¾-inches long, and the smaller is around 2½ inches long. The prices run about $200 for either size, but rare woods or ivory will up the cost another $100. The one wood that has caused the most excitement is pink ivory, a wood from the royal trees of the Zulus. It is found in the bushveld regions of Zululand, Swaziland, Mozambique, the Transvaal, and Botswana. Since 1967 any damage to the species has been forbidden in the Bantu territories of South Africa. In that country the wood is known as red ivory and has been called the "wood that is rarer than diamonds." It is almost impossible to obtain and may be cut only by a Zulu chief or his sons. When a young man cuts a tree and fashions a spear, he is said to have reached manhood. Even today among the Zulu only tribal chieftains are permitted to possess knobkerries (a form of club) made of red ivory, and the rarity of the wood makes it very desirable for small knife handles. Herron has one piece weighing slightly over twelve pounds and how he obtained it is a story in itself. A nearby dealer in exotic woods called one day and said he had a piece of unusual wood that would make good knife handles. The dealer had already been in touch with the department of forestry in Pretoria and knew what he had. Herron paid as much for this one piece of wood as he would have for an equal amount of ivory. It was a good investment and makes a superb handle. The wood is solid and hard, although it takes a year or more to season properly, and can be polished to a beautiful smooth finish. Its brilliant pink color makes a most attractive addition to any knife. How did such a large piece of a protected tree find its way to this country? Well, as the story goes, a couple of adventurers killed a

Zulu guard, hacked down a tree, chopped it into small chunks, and smuggled it out of the country. True or not, it makes a romantic tale, and the legend of intrigue plus the rareness of the wood have made it highly desirable among knife enthusiasts. In fact, wood collectors—and they are just as fanatical as knife collectors—have offered enormous sums to Herron just for a small sample piece.

But pink ivory isn't the only rarity offered by Herron. African blackwood is equally desirable and is a deep jet black that will, as it ages, show swirls of grain that reflect as the material is turned in the light. Other woods kept in stock are rosewood, cocobolo, osage orange, walnut burl, and many others. Stag is in fairly short supply, and ivory is becoming more expensive. Like other knifemen, Herron keeps a goodly supply of Micartas on hand and feels, as do the other experts, that it probably makes the best knife handle of all. Of course, the collector of the rare and unusual wouldn't think of settling for something as mundane as Micarta, and for those who seek the ultimate, pink ivory will suffice until a large enough gemstone is found that would make an all-diamond handle.

As to steels, Herron, after trying almost everything in the book, uses Crucible's 154-CM exclusively. Although he prefers this steel, he hesitates to recommend it for the amateur. There are many other steels that fashion into a good knife and probably will be a bit easier for the beginner. Most knifemakers started with O-1, and A-2 makes an excellent knife. Herron said, "If I were to make a few knives for myself I'd probably use A-2, knowing what I do about steel. It's easy to grind, simple to polish, and it's fairly easy to get it heat-treated since most small-sized towns have a machine shop that do their own heat-treating."

Asked the reason why many knifemakers offer so many different steels, Herron responds that many of their customers are frequently more knowledgeable about steels than the makers themselves. Some prefer a carbon steel knife in the belief it is easier to sharpen and stainless steels have gotten a bad rap, since most people think of cheap kitchen knives that won't hold an edge. Herron, like other knifemen, prefers to get away from the term "stainless" and says that "corrosion-resistant makes more sense."

Herron prefers to use one type of steel since it keeps his operation simpler without too many different types of steels about the shop to confuse him and his heat-treater when the knives are sent off. He recounted instances of some craftsmen having their blades mixed up at the treating plant, going through the wrong process, and losing a batch of perfectly good blades.

On handle materials for the amateur, Herron obviously is prejudiced toward woods. "Wood is easy to work and makes the most beautiful handles." The amateur will find wood easy to shape on either a grinding belt or with hand files. For a knife that is going to be put to hard use, Micarta is Herron's choice and he considers it the most sensible material to use. For the average sporting use of a knife, a wood handle will still last a lifetime, and if the knife is given some care, probably several lifetimes and may be passed down to a son and to his sons, too.

The biggest expense in making a few knives will be heat-treating. The blank itself will probably run $3 or $4 and handle material and pins or rivets plus a piece of fiber liner will run another $5 or $6, but heat treating for one blade alone could run high, depending on the shop used. Of course, the more knives sent, the lower the cost. That's one reason most knifemakers send at least a dozen blades at one time. If there is a friendly knifemaker in the neighborhood, Herron's advice is to ask him to include your blade along with the next batch he sends out. That way the price would probably run a couple of dollars. But this isn't to be considered an open invitation to begin sending blades to every knifemaker.

Making the Folding Knife

Keep in mind from the beginning that it takes George Herron about twenty hours to craft each folder. This includes making every piece, along with grinding, polishing, and fitting. It does not include the time allowed for sending the blade off for heat-treating nor can the time taken by Uncle Sam for delivery be included, but the actual labor is about twenty hours. A talented amateur might double this while someone less skilled may run sixty or more hours. Naturally, there is no speed contest involved and the amateur should work slowly, with care and careful attention to fitting each small part and exercising exceptional caution with grinding belts and buffing wheels.

As a professional, Herron works with groups of parts. That is, he may make fifty blades, an equal number of locking bars, and everything else required to assemble at least that many knives. This actually cuts down on the time required for set-up in making each piece. This will take a better part of a week; then the blades are sent off for heat-treatment. When everything is returned, Herron will pick up a blade and locking bar that have already been fitted and begin making the knife. This doesn't mean that everything falls into place. Some pieces may fit better than others while some may require additional filing or fitting. On occasion, a particular knife will be almost completed when a scale will crack; then the craftsman must back up a couple of hours and do the work over again.

The work must proceed slowly at this stage since errors can be time-consuming. Crafting a folder is more difficult than making a regular sheath knife; each piece must fit exactly and work well against other parts. Holes must be aligned with care and precision so the pins go through. If everything is not exact at this point, the knife just won't work. I hope the photographs I've included here will be self-explanatory, but the steps required will be outlined so that the beginning knifemaker may refer back to any particular area that may be confusing.

The first step is making the blade and locking bar. Once this is done, a hole is drilled and reamed for the pivot pin or bushing that Herron uses. When this hole is drilled it is used as a reference point all the way through making the blade and locking bar. Once the rough blank is ground out to profile on a 60-grit belt, the bevels will be ground out. The notch for the locking bar is cut on a milling machine, but it can be done by file. While filing is a slower process, it will give just as good a fit and, in fact, Herron admits that once the cut is made on the milling machine, he uses small files to smoooth off tiny burrs and milling marks anyway.

The next step is also done by the milling machine, and that is putting in the nail nick. This can be done with a chisel or hand-ground in with a small stone formed to the shape of the nail nick.

The hole is now drilled in the locking bar. Go back to the 60-grit belt grinder and grind to the dimensions. These two pieces require heat-treating, but are the major pieces of the folder. 154-CM steel is used for the locking bar as well as for the blade, and both are treated to RC 61 or 62.

The next step is to make the liners. The liners are 304 stainless steel. Two

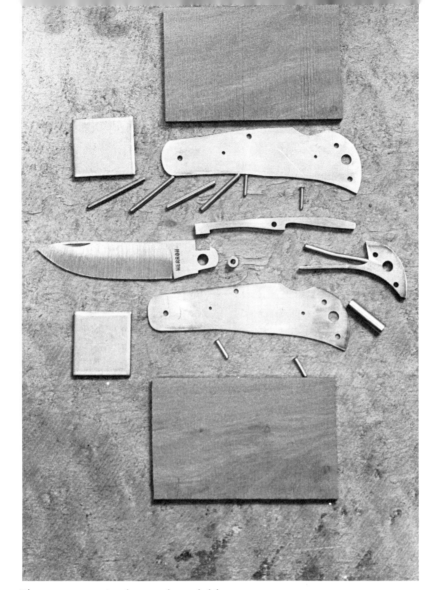

The parts required to make a folder.

A blade is profiled onto a piece of 440-C using a template.

A hole is drilled and reamed for the pivot pin.

Cutting out the blade with a slow-speed bandsaw.

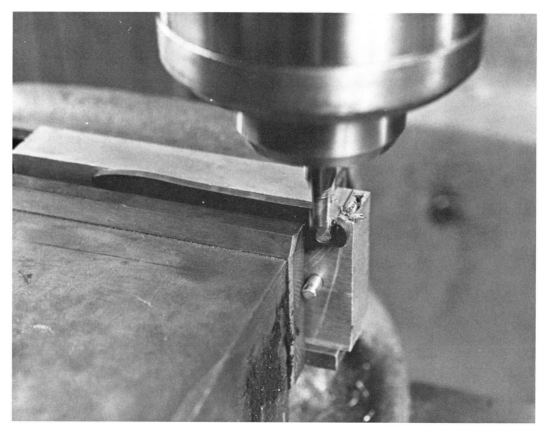

Cutting the notch for the locking bar. Although this is being done on a milling machine, it can also be done with files.

Cutting the nail nick on the milling machine.

Smoothing out burrs and milling marks with a fine file.

Checking the fit of a locking bar and notch.

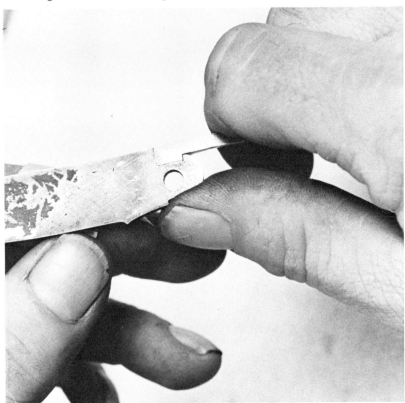

sets of liners are clamped together and holes are drilled so that they will line up precisely. Here Herron uses assembly pins to put everything together for fit. Once assured that everything fits properly, Herron grinds the two liners down to the shape of the knife.

At this stage the spring or spring holder is cut out. This fits into the knife. Once again the small brass assembly pins are used to put everything together to check fit. At this point, if everything checks out, Herron moves on to the next step, which is the bushing.

In Herron's folding knives the blade pivots on a bushing of 174-CH stainless steel. This particular steel is heat-treated locally to about RC 35 to 38. The bushing is about 0.001 or 0.002 wider than the blade, and this allows the maker to peen the ends down without locking the blade. The main reason for the bushing liner is to take any wear off the pivot pin.

Assuming that everything works well, the bolsters are now put on the liners. The bolsters are 304 stainless steel. An undercut is put on the bolsters on the Square Wheel grinder with a platen set at 45°. Hard silver solder is used to solder the bolster to the liner. The bolster is ground down with a 60-grit belt.

The handle scales or covers are cut slightly oversize and placed on the grinder for a 45° cut at one end so that it will fit into the 45° cut on the bolster. The hole is cut through the bolster for the pivot pin. Again check out each step.

Now Herron is ready to glue the handle material to the liner with an industrial epoxy. Some craftsmen only use pins; Herron prefers to use both pins and epoxy. The pins are stainless steel. Once the epoxy is allowed to set for at least a day, the handle material is ground down. Now it begins to look like a knife.

Holes are drilled for the pins. The bolster is turned upside down and the holes already in the liners are used as a guide for drilling through the handle material. Now is the time to roughly assemble the knife once again, take a good look at it, and make certain that everything works smoothly and well. Grind excess material off everything with a 60-grit belt. Everything is shaped down roughly with progressively finer belts. Although the knife is still held together with temporary pins, Herron works down to a 220-grit belt, and this gives a decent finish on the blade and locking bar.

Then the knife is disassembled and the working parts of the knife are polished. The liners are ground down on a 220-grit belt, then 400-grit, and a well-worked 600-grit belt with buffing compound. The inside of the liners are mirror-finished on the buffing wheels.

At this stage the knife is now ready for final assembly. Herron feels that this is the most critical part of knifemaking. The final pins are cut and the knife is again put together for a last check.

The stainless steel pins are cut perhaps 0.003 or 0.004 longer and the pins are peened down. With ivory, gentle taps are necessary; with Micarta, perhaps a slightly heavier hand can be used with the peening hammer. Once all the pins are tapped down, a file is used to cut the rough ends down even with the bolsters and handle. At this stage a lanyard liner is then put in. This is a piece of stainless steel tubing that is epoxied in and gently flared or peened down so that it won't move. A smooth-cut mill file is used to file the shape of the handle down to pretty exact shape. Then use a piece of 320-grit emery paper, wet or dry, to take out all the file marks.

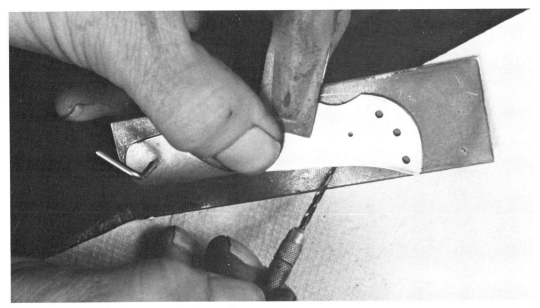

Profiles of the liners are made from the template.

The liners are assembled with pins. If everything fits, both liners are ground down to the shape of the knife.

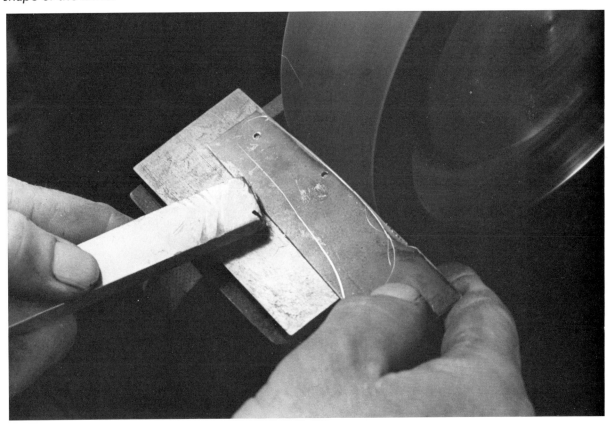

Next, the spring or spring holder is cut out.

Again, the pieces are put together with a pin to check the fit.

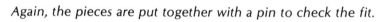

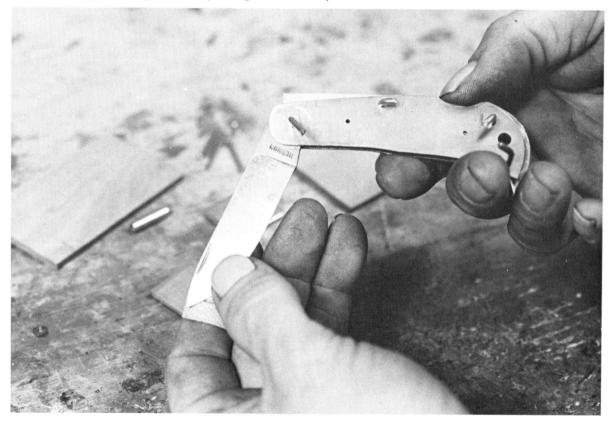

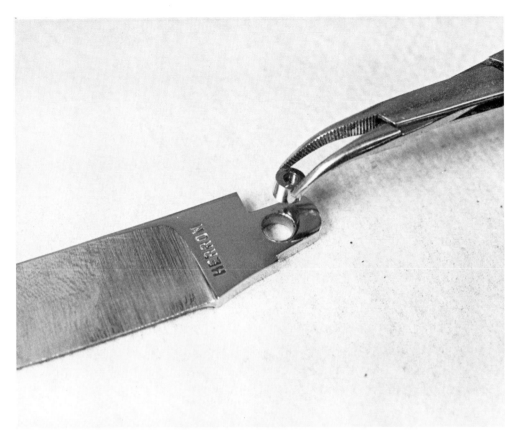

The blade pivots on a bushing of 174-CH stainless steel, and this is set into the bushing hole.

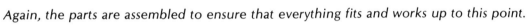

Again, the parts are assembled to ensure that everything fits and works up to this point.

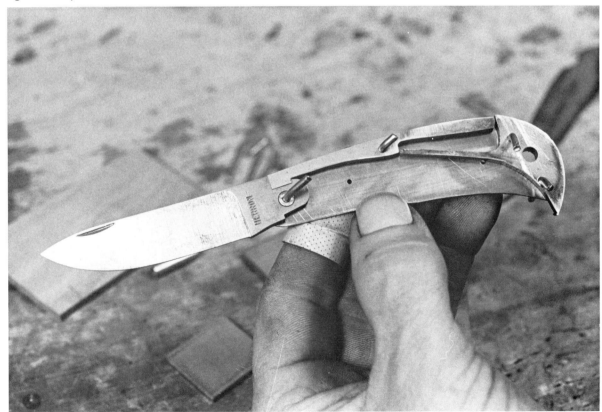

Close-up of the undercut bolster that will next be soldered onto the liner.

The 45° undercut bolster is clamped to a liner and soldered in place.

Bolster being ground down to fit with a 60-grit belt. The bolsters are 304 stainless steel, and hard silver solder is used to solder the bolster to the liner.

Close-up of a bolster partially formed on the grinder.

Bolsters completely shaped and ready for the pink ivory covers.

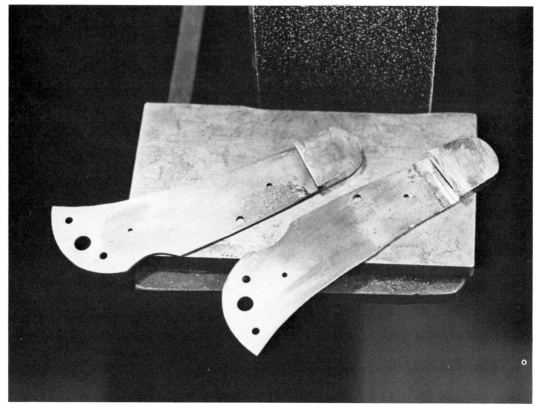

The pink ivory slabs for the covers are sanded flat with the Sears flat sander.

With the platen set at a 45° angle, the ends of the covers are ground to fit against the bolsters.

After epoxy is applied, the wooden cover is clamped to the liner and allowed to dry overnight.

Once the epoxy has hardened, the various pin holes are drilled.

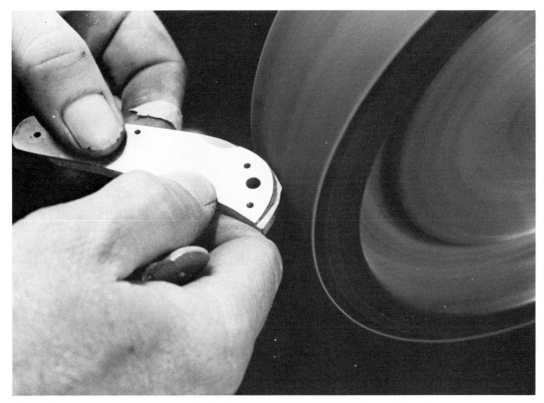

Now the wood covers are sanded down to match the outline of the liners.

The blade has been polished and the knife is once again assembled with pins. Herron feels that this is the most important part of knifemaking, and that everything should fit and work smoothly.

The various pins are gently peened down and flared very slightly.

The lanyard hole is lined with a piece of stainless steel tubing. It is epoxyed in place and then gently flared or peened out to prevent its moving.

The final step is to sharpen the blade. While many knifemen sharpen on belts, Herron's advice for the amateur is to use stones. Here Herron uses a Norton oil cradle with three different grits kept in oil at the bottom of the cradle.

115

The knife is now ready for finishing the blade. Again a 60-grit belt is used to remove all excess metal. Progress to the 220, 400, 500, and 500 with buffing compound. Herron uses three different grades of buffing compound. First is Lea 316, the coarsest compound; next is Lea 309; then finish with Lea's 312, a scratch-free compound giving the high mirror finish to the blade. Depending on the handle material used, Herron may then go to the Lea 316. This is a greasy compound; some handle materials will absorb the material and it will be difficult to remove. Herron uses a commercial degreaser to remove all compound from the knife, a few drops of oil are placed on the moving parts, and the blade is opened and closed a few times to work the oil in.

The final step is to sharpen the knife. A professional knifemaker will usually sharpen on belts, but Herron's advice for the amateur is to use stones. It may take a little more time, but it allows the craftsman to think a bit while he's working. While Herron uses both methods, he admits that throughout his knifemaking career, he has preferred to sharpen knives by hand and use a Norton oil cradle—although any good stones may be used.

Again, buffing is the most hazardous operation in knifemaking. This is the reason Herron refuses to buff and polish a blade that's already sharpened. The amateur should exercise caution, also.

Making the Tapered-Tang Hunting Knife

From the extreme of the most exacting knife, the folder, let's move on to a fairly simple knife, a tapered-tang hunting knife with slab handles. This is Herron's Little Dude, one of the most popular knives in his catalog. For the amateur craftsman it is an easy knife to make. Basically, a small piece of steel is ground to shape with the handle slabs and fastened with epoxy and rivets.

There are probably fewer steps in crafting a knife of this type than any other. The steps are as follows. Cut out the blank on the bandsaw once the outline is scribed out. Move over to the drill press and drill the holes for the rivets. Go to the grinder and profile the blade using a 60-grit belt and get down to good, clean metal until the exact outline of the knife is visible. Then the center of the blade is marked as reference points for rough-grinding. Next the rough bevels are ground in with a 60-grit belt. Using the same machine (Bader or Square Wheel), rough-grind or taper the tang. Once the steel is removed, put the platen on and taper or flatten the tang. This is where the maker gets a true, flat taper. Be sure to go from the front of the tang to the back of the tang, leaving the end roughly 1/16 inch thick. At this point, other than stamping his name, Herron is through with the knife until after heat-treating.

Once the blade is returned, polish both the blade and the ricasso area, which obviously cannot be reached once the slabs are put on. Select the handle material, lay the blade handle on, and mark an outline with a pencil. Move to the bandsaw and rough-cut the slabs. Next, holes are drilled by clamping the slabs, one at a time, to the tang and drilling the holes with the same-size drill that was used for the tang holes. The outside of the slab holes are slightly counterbored for the blind screws that are used. Care should be taken to set the drill press so that the counterbore is not too deep. Otherwise, it is possible to go right through the hole and the handle is lost. Next a piece of liner material is cut to rough size and

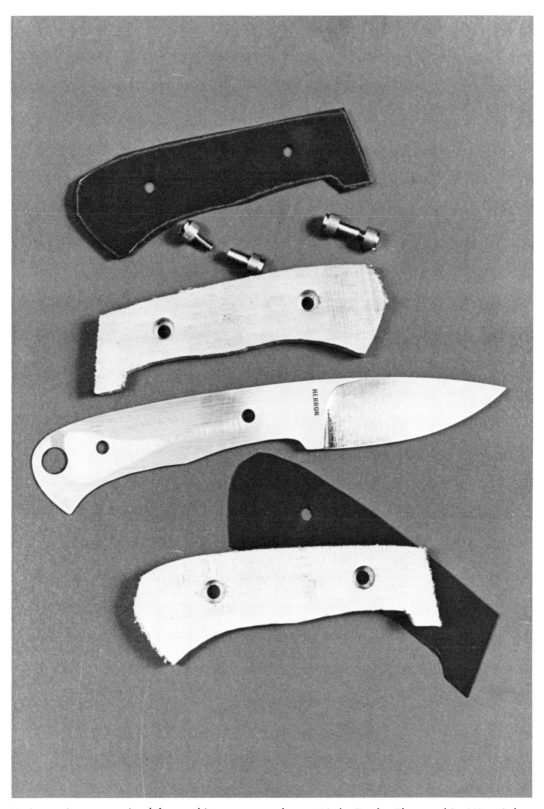

Various pieces required for making a tapered-tang Little Dude. The steel is 440 stainless and the wooden blanks for the handles are osage orange.

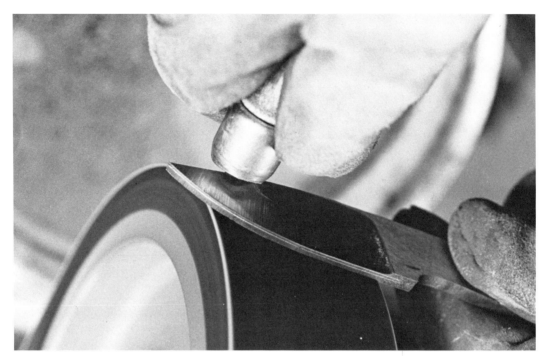

After the profile has been cut with a bandsaw, the blade is shaped on a 60-grit belt. Note the edge lines scribed out.

With the platen attached, the tang is tapered. Note the use of a small metal push rod.

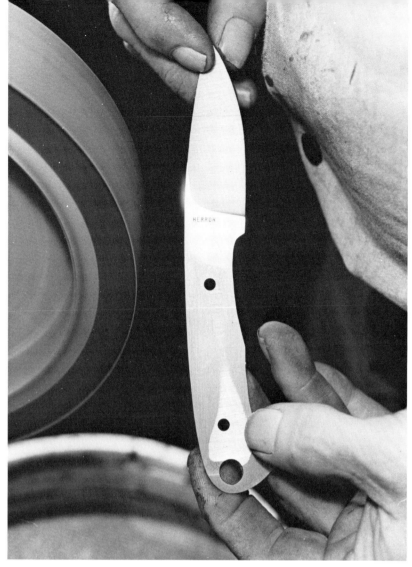

Once the blade is returned from heat-treating, polish the blade, the ricasso area, and do the final tapering of the tang.

After the final blade grinding, an industrial degreaser is used to clean the blade.

Cutting a piece of osage orange for the handles.

Once the slabs are cut, an outline is made for cutting on the bandsaw.

Clamped to the steel tang, the rivet holes are drilled out of the handle slabs.

The outsides of the holes are then counterbored for the blind screws or rivets that are used.

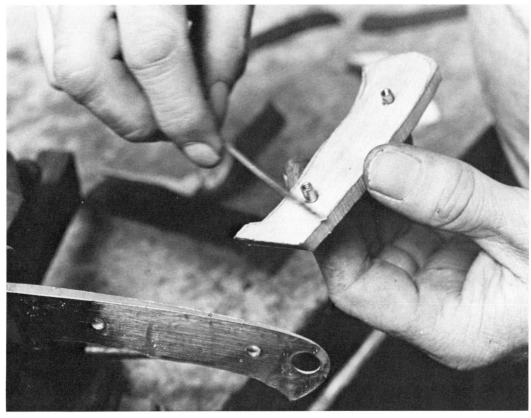

Epoxy is spread over both pieces of wood to hold the fiber liner material, and then the tang is covered with epoxy.

is placed together with both slabs and liners to check fit. Grind it down to size, making certain that the screws and everything else fit properly.

Prepare the epoxy and coat all four pieces, two liners, and both handle slabs. Assemble together with screws and even tighten down with a couple of C clamps. Allow to set overnight. At present the knife looks pretty crude, so excess handle material is removed with the 60-grit belt on the Square Wheel grinder. Grind down to the metal all around the handle, then grind off the excess on the sides. Once this is done, place the knife in a clamp on the workbench and file the handle down to shape. The first filing is done with a coarse file; then move on to a finer file as the handle begins to take shape. Once the handle is almost shaped, take a piece of 100-grit emery paper and hand-sand the wood to remove all file marks.

Move to the belt again and use a 320 grit to finish up the metal tang area. Back to the bench and finish up with a 320-grit wet or dry paper and finish by hand. The handle is now ready for buffing while the blade must be ground, removing excess metal. Prepare to finish the shape and polish the blade.

To finish the blade, begin with a 60-grit belt, next 220, 400, and 500, with buffing compound on the buffing wheel. Again, as with the folder, the same procedure is used: Lea 316, 309, and 312 compound. It may be necessary to go back to the finer-grit belt on the grinder to remove a scratch, but once this is done the

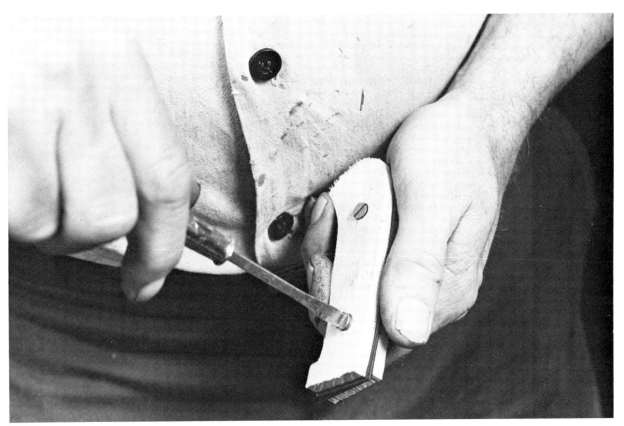

All four pieces are tightened down with the screws and allowed to dry overnight.

Rough-shaping of the wooden handle slabs with the 60-grit belt.

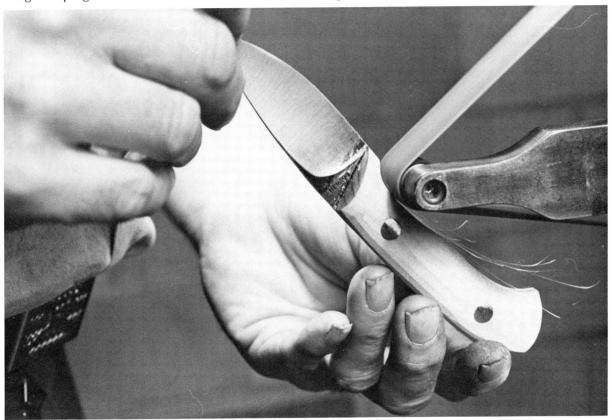

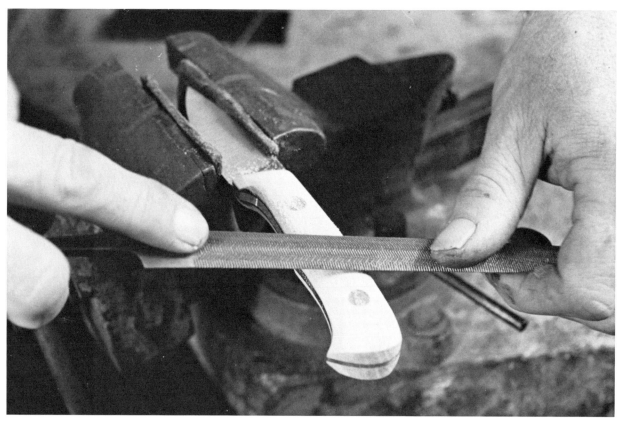

Once the rough sanding is done, the knife is placed in the vise and taken down with finer files and then with emery paper.

The two completed knives.

knife is completed. Of course, the knife must be cleaned with degreaser, sharpened, and a sheath must be made.

Although this may seem like a great many steps, the work goes fairly fast. If care is taken, the reward will be a good-looking, practical hunting knife.

The machinery required by the amateur knifemaker can be relatively simple. One good grinder can be used to both shape and profile a blade completely, and Herron feels that for the beginner, a bandsaw isn't even necessary. A hand drill can be used for drilling the various holes for pins and rivets, and a hacksaw or hand saw will cut the handle materials. The basic piece of equipment required is a good Bader or Square Wheel or Burr King grinder. If a man doesn't want to invest in a buffer, he can leave the blade alone once the final 500-grit belt is used with buffing compound. He won't get as high a polish, but if it's a using knife, it really won't matter.

On occasion some amateur craftsmen have used a small buffing wheel on a hand drill and this will work well if too many knives aren't made.

George Herron feels that if the novice knifemaker improvises he will find that all the expensive machinery isn't required.

9

LLOYD HALE:
THE BOWIE KNIFE

If knowledgeable collectors have a list of favorite knifemakers, Lloyd Hale would certainly be among the top names. Hale is deep into the realm of art knives and regards himself as a sculptor of steel and wood rather than a knifemaker.

Despite his romance with knives, Hale has little interest in blades themselves, and aside from the usual household cutlery, there are no knives in his home. Asked to explain this, Hale responded, "People get hurt with knives, and I've been injured enough making knives to give them proper respect." In spite of that Hale literally eats, sleeps, and lives knives—not as cutting objects, but rather as a piece of art, something made of raw material that will be beautiful enough to please him and delight his clients.

Asked where his far-out ideas come from, Hale replied, "Everywhere. When I'm fishing, listening to music, at the movies, or watching television, ideas are constantly running through my mind."

Not strange for an artist either is Hale's desire to have his knives live on long after he's departed the scene. In fact, the first blades he ever saw impressed him mightily. A meeting with California bowie authority Bill Williamson exposed him to magnificent hand-crafted knives of our early history. These were push daggers, small dirks, and some rare old bowies crafted by Michael Price and Will and Finck, early cutlers of San Francisco's Gold Rush era. "The thought that these knives were collected by someone today just blew my mind. I knew that's what I wanted to do, make something that would live on after I'm gone."

Also rare among modern knifemakers is Hale's pricing structure, as unusual as his philosophy. He rarely takes an order for a specific knife, but asks what the customer wants to spend. An $800 knife will receive that much work and a

$2,000 blade will be more decorative. One of his biggest orders ran about $5,000, with an average bowie costing around $1,500.

Although Hale began with hunting knives, and he still occasionally makes one for a friend, his first love is highly decorative blades—and the more ornate the better.

After putting in time as a resident knifesmith at Black's Forge in Washington, Arkansas, Hale moved to Springdale when knifemaker Bob Dozier left Morseth Knives and Hale filled the slot. Hale admits to learning good working habits while at Morseth, and now that he has his own shop, he is usually in the shop at 6 A.M. and puts in a fairly long day.

Asked what skills the new knifeman should have, Hale replies, "The eyes to see and the desire to make a knife." But the problem remains how to get the steel off the blank so that the knife is left. Hale feels that patience is probably the greatest asset for any beginner, saying: "Most aspiring knifemakers run out of patience too soon. All the grinding, sanding, and polishing discourages them before a third of the work is completed."

Steel, always a subject for controversy, is 440-C for most of Hale's collector's knives and A-2 is the choice for a using knife.

In spite of his fine reputation, Hale hasn't been making knives that long. He only began in 1969, but his skills would be considered high-paying in any other enterprise. An early turn at Alcan gave him the expertise to work metal. Always skilled with his hands, Hale has made pistol grips, gun stocks, and even guitars.

When it comes to making a knife, Hale works in the widely accepted stock-removal method. He is also a meticulous craftsman and proceeds with exacting care. One rule: when the shop door opens, all work ceases. "I'm a nut on this," Hale remarked, "I can't work and visit at the same time and I won't try." That was the only example of temperament shown by Hale and it's easy to understand.

For his blade grind Hale finds the flat grind the best for the type of blade he makes. In fact, Hale said, "There is a lot of mystique about the flat grind. Some makers who do it well like to make a mystery about it when, in fact, it's the easiest grind to do. The show knife, or collector's piece, shows this grind off to best advantage, but for a hunting knife it can be the worst kind of grind, since it offers a wedge blade and the only thin place is the cutting edge. The hollow grind, on the other hand, starts high on the blade and stays thin to the edge." On the English-style bowie he feels the flat grind is correct; on the American type, the hollow grind is better because, as Hale says, "The flat type tends not to look right."

For his file work Hale uses a large variety of sizes and shapes. He begins with a standard 3/4-inch file 6 inches in length. His round files are chain-saw files that can be purchased in most hardware stores. For intricate work he uses imported Swiss files, some as small as needles. The latter are used on nickle silver tips and throats of sheaths as well as on the same material on guards and butt caps. But before beginning any file work, Hale admonishes the craftsman to sit down and think about what he plans to do. Oddly enough, many of Hale's ideas come from visits to antique shops that have old furniture or from viewing old buildings. These are full of spirals and curves and lead to some excellent ideas for knife decor. With all the clamor for his highly decorated blades, Hale's fancy work didn't begin until late 1973. First working the spine of the blade, he gradually moved out to the guard

As with all knifemaking, a piece of steel is painted with Bykem and the profile of the blade scribed on with a sharp metal scriber.

and butt and, much later, realized that the tang had possibilities, too. What are the tools Hale uses to accomplish all this? He has a variable-speed bandsaw along with a Burr King belt sander, two Baldor buffers, a drill press, a couple of vises, and enough files to stock a hardware store.

Like many knifemen, Hale has discovered little tricks that work best for him. For example, he uses a commercial product called Cryocut as a lubricant on the bandsaw blades. It doesn't smoke or smell like oil, and Hale likes it so much he even uses it on drilling and grinding operations.

But let's join Hale as he makes a show bowie. First he marks the profile of the blade after painting the blank with lay-out fluid. This is used by almost all knife-makers and can be obtained at industrial supply houses. It is called Bykem and comes in cans or spray. To cut the profiled blank he uses the slowest speed on the bandsaw, 100 feet per minute, and then grinds the profile down with a well-used 36-grit sanding belt. Once that is done, Hale flattens the blade on the Sears 6 x 48 flat grinder. The next step is to lay out the location where the double guard goes onto the blade and file any decoration along the spine. Bear in mind that all file work must be done before the blade is heat-treated; otherwise, it will be too hard to file later. With the fancy file work, Hale says, "Use your imagination and put your body into it." Plus a couple of words of caution, "Don't push or bear down too hard. I've broken more files and scraped more knuckles because I tried to hurry and speed up my filing." When the filing is completed, the blade is cleaned on a 120-grit Bright Boy rubber wheel, running at 1,725 rpm. Next comes a little buffing on a medium felt wheel using black stainless compound.

Now for the pregrind, as Hale calls it. This is done on the 2-by-8 contact

When cutting out the profile, Hale uses the slowest speed on the bandsaw, 100 fpm. Cryo-cut makes an excellent lubricant and does not smoke or smell.

Hale flattens the profile blank on the Sears 6 x 48 flat grinder.

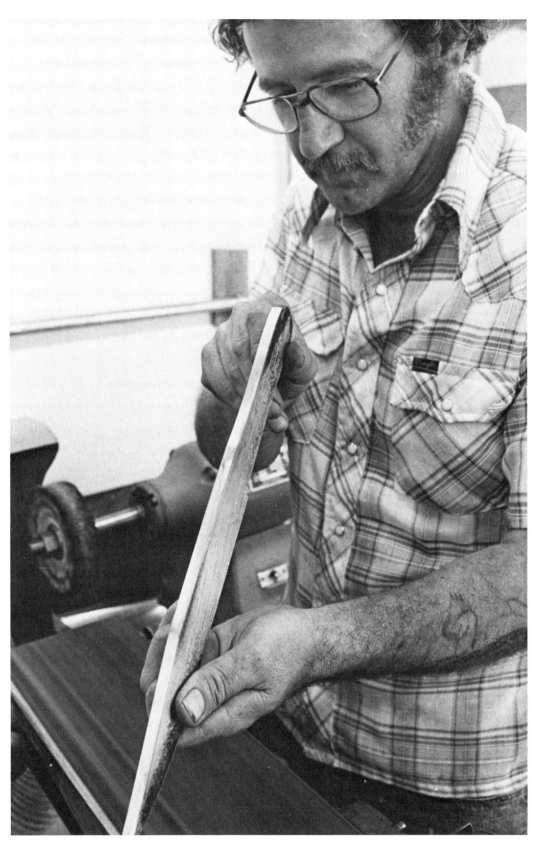

Hale checks the trueness of the blank by eye.

Hale lays out the location where the double guard goes onto the blade and does any decorative file work necessary before heat-treating.

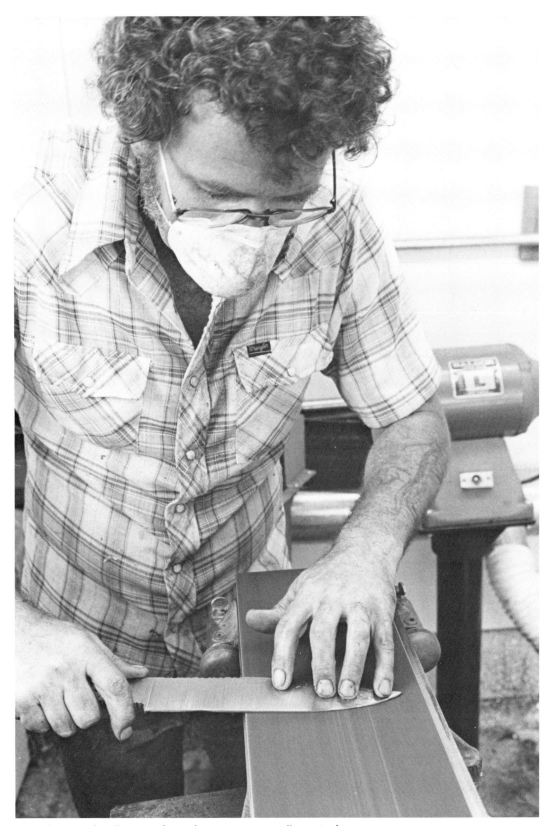

Hale begins the flat grind on the Sears 6 x 48 flat grinder.

The flat grind is continued on the contact wheel of the Burr King grinder. A sheet of 220-grit Carborundum paper is cemented to the wheel and then cut off for a perfect circle.

wheel, on the Burr King. This grinder will remove metal fast, but at this point, Hale isn't too concerned with a true flat grind. Next he moves over to the 6 x 48 flat sander and begins flattening the blade with the 60-grit belt. During all these operations Hale never wears gloves. "I have to feel what's going on, or in this case, what's coming off." The next step is to drill a number of holes in the tang to give proper balance and move over to the 220-grit belt for a rough polish. Then the blade is ready for heat-treating.

Hale is one of a small group of knifemakers who do their own heat-treating; he uses a Cress electric furnace that sells for about $500. For those who may eventually want to do their own heat-treating, the following description and techniques are for 440-C only. "The most important thing is to pack the floor of the chamber with charcoal briquettes to eat up oxygen during heat-treating," says Hale. Once this is done, place the blade in the chamber and slowly bring the temperature to 1,950° F. When the temperature is reached, remove the blade and allow it to air-quench for 15 to 20 minutes, and then freeze it with dry ice for an hour. Be prepared for some unholy wails when the ice hits the metal. The sound can be pretty terrifying and resembles two prehistoric monsters fighting in some oozing, primeval swamp. When the hour is up, the blade can now be double-drawn in an oven at 450°F, allowing it to cool to room temperature between each draw.

After the final draw, Hale advises caution with the subsequent steps, saying: "This is the most dangerous time in knifemaking, and if your mind isn't into it, go pester your wife. Do anything, but don't work on knives." Hale admits to

The blade is now fairly close to the required dimensions and is finished on the contact wheel.

A number of holes are drilled in the tang to give the proper balance; then the piece is rough-polished on the 220-grit belt and placed in the Cress electric oven.

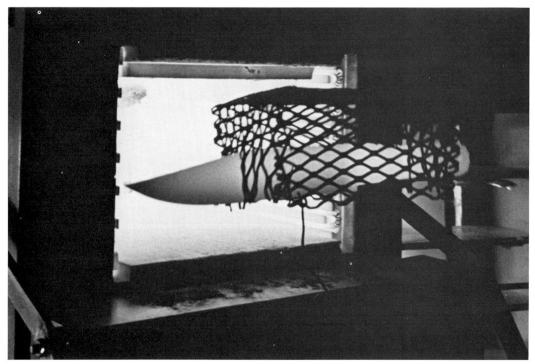

Out of the oven and allowed to cool for 15 to 20 minutes, then packed in dry ice.

ruining more good blades at this point because he wasn't ready. He has also been badly injured because some idea hasn't jelled or an irate customer stalked into his shop to upset the day. It's also the time when Hale swears every machine in his shop is waiting for him with sharp teeth and honed talons . . . just looking for that first mistake.

Once again it's back to the 6-by-48 flat sander with a 60-grit belt to finish grinding. Take care to do it evenly and pay particular attention to getting the back of the bevels even using the side of the belt for bevels. The technique is to track the belt slightly off the edge and push up against the belt. Next use a 9-inch round disc sander. Take a standard 9-inch-square 220-grit Carborundum paper and cement this to the round wheel; cut off the excess so that it's perfectly round. The 200 grit is used to remove scratches left by the 60 grit. After all scratches are removed, go to 320 and 400 grits. When these steps are completed, finish with a 600 grit. Move on to the 8-inch buffing wheel and be generous with Green Chrome compound. Buff in all directions and hold tightly to the blade so that it can't be torn from the hands. Practice will show the correct amount of pressure to be applied, since it's possible to change bevel angles just by buffing. Again, keep a bucket of water handy for cooling the blade because the buffing wheel can generate tremendous heat. When the blade is completed, cover it with masking tape to protect the polish and move on to the next steps.

With the blade completed, the hardware is prepared for the guard and handle. Nickle silver is cut to size, then drilled with a series of 1/16-inch holes. These will be filed open to fit over the tang perfectly. This is another period in knifemaking when filing and fitting will take time and patience; so don't despair too quickly. Once the guard is filed and fits perfectly, it is ready for the decorative file work.

The 200-grit belt is used to remove any scratches left by 60 grit. When all scratches are removed, go on to 320 and 400 grits. When these steps are completed, finish with the 600-grit belt.

Surprisingly, Hale never lays out his file work, preferring to go freehand. In spite of this, he admits it all comes out in the end. In fact, Hale says, "Some of my finest patterns were created to accommodate a bad ending. Collectors look at it and say, 'Boy, that's wild! Wonder where he got the idea?' Well, I'll tell you. He got it because he didn't want to scrap the damn thing and start over."

To continue, drill a hole at each end of the guard the size of the pins to be used. Slot the two thin pieces, scribe around the edges of the main centerpiece, and grind off the excess. Rivet the three pieces of the guard together; then use a 400 and a 600 grit to clean off the front and back using a disc sander.

Now the liners and bolster are prepared for the stag handles or scales. Cut a thin piece of nickle silver and solder it to a 3/8-inch nickle silver bar. Hale uses a medium silver solder that flows at 1,200 degrees for this step. Butt this against the guard, already on the knife, then drill 1/16-inch holes for pins and scribe out the handle. A sharp file is used to cut the design into the edge of the liner, then a small chisel is used to cut the design into the soft metal. With this, Hale says: "Use your imagination. There are unlimited numbers of patterns and designs—just think!"

The liner, with 3/8-inch nickle silver bolster soldered on, is flattened against the anvil with hammer taps, and both pieces of stag are ground to flatness. Holes

136

When using the 8-inch buffing wheel, be generous with Green Chrome buffing compound. Once this task is complete, completely cover the blade with masking tape to protect the polish.

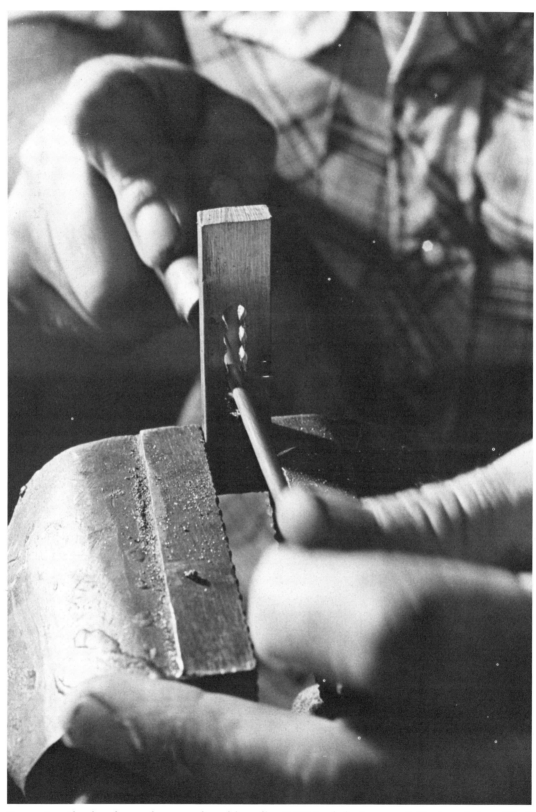

Preparing the hardware for guard and handle; 1/16-inch holes are drilled and then filed for a perfect fit.

Trying the fit of the nickle silver guard on the tang.

Beginning to file the decorative work on the nickle silver guard.

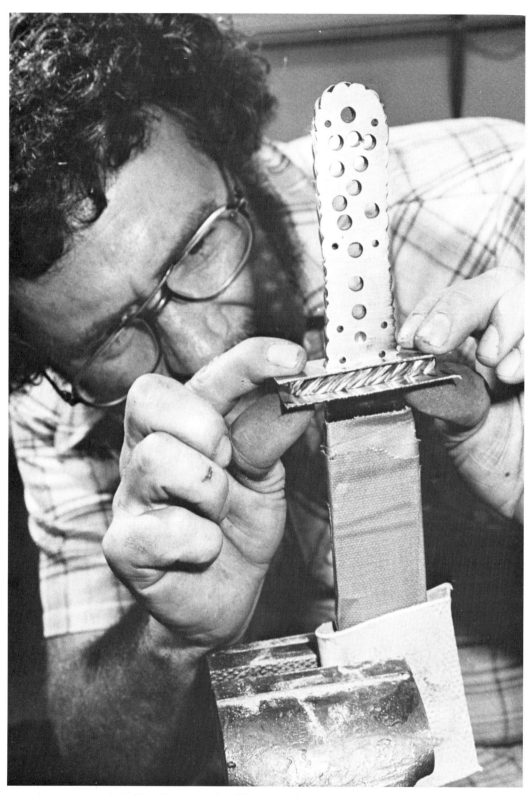

Two thin pieces of nickle silver are also filed and then riveted onto the guard by two pins, one at each end. Note the tape-wrapped blade and the piece of fiber used in the vise to prevent any marks on the polished blade.

140

The two thin pieces are peened down and . . .

. . . then sanded smooth on the round disk sander.

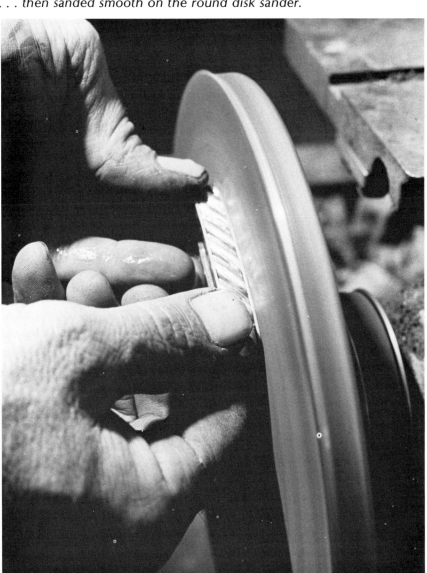

Preparing the liners and bolsters. Cut a thin piece of nickle silver and solder it to a 3/8-inch nickle silver bar. Hale uses a medium silver solder that flows at 1,200°F.

The edges of the thin nickle silver liners are cut with a chisel for decoration.

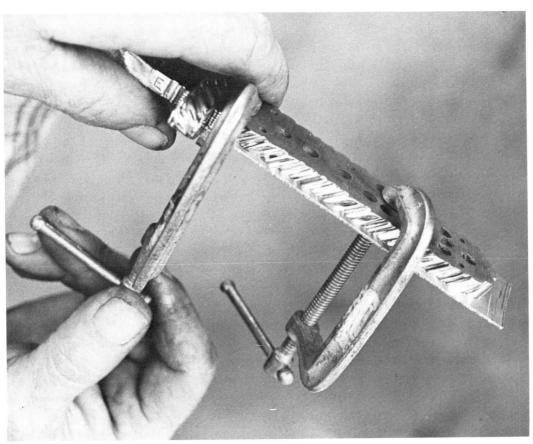

Once the nickle silver liners and bolster have been soldered, they are butted up tight against the guard and 1/16-inch holes drilled for pins.

The cut-to-size pieces of stag are flattened on the Sears 6 x 28 flat grinder for a smooth fit onto the liners.

The pins are gently peened down with light hammer taps.

are drilled, nickle silver pins cut slightly oversize to allow a small amount of peening, and the entire handle is completed with pins hammered down with light taps. "What you have now," says Hale with a grin, "is one sorta fancy, flat-ground bowie."

Perhaps the most important point, at least from Hale's point of view, is never to lose your sense of humor. "Crafting knives is a demanding occupation, but the self-satisfaction is tremendous," he claims. "When you've done a beautiful job and it's come out the way you planned, it's the greatest feeling in the world."

144

The completed bowie and fine case.

10

BILL MORAN: THE MASTER OF DAMASCUS

Damascus is defined in the dictionary as a type of steel with a wavy or variegated pattern made by welding iron and steel for the crafting of sword blades.

Thought originally to have been made in the Middle East at Damascus in Syria, most steel of this type actually came from Persia or India and, in fact, had been used for centuries by such disparate races as the Japanese and Vikings.

Invariably, the first question put by a viewer of a fine Damascus blade is how the wavy pattern was put into the blade. Actually, it is the grain of the metal itself brought out by etching with acid, but the grain was worked into the metal by the heat of the forge and the layers of welded steel and iron. Some of Moran's blades have as many as 250 layers, with a few going as high as a thousand, but the best knives run about 512 layers and offer the most eye-catching patterns for the collector. The blades have an individual character and personality as different as each human being, and Bill, like most artist-craftsmen, feels that a part of his own personality goes into each blade he makes. And so it has been with armourers throughout history.

Why Damascus blades stopped being made is probably lost in the mists of time. Moran feels that the skills were too difficult, and it became easier to make a blade from a single piece of steel. Economics probably played a part, too. Says Moran, "There must be those who are willing to pay the artisan's price for creating works of art, and throughout history there were periods when the right circumstances prevailed and great artwork was produced." In spite of our present-day economy, there are still those willing to pay for fine quality, for pieces of art that will be the treasures of the future.

How difficult is it to produce a Damascus blade? Moran says, "Difficult beyond belief. So much so that forging any other blade is simplicity itself. For ex-

Two of Bill Moran's fine forged knives. Both are made of Damascus steel.

The hammers and tools of the blacksmith.

ample, it takes 125 pounds of high-grade coal to forge one Damascus blade, whereas an ordinary blade can be forged with about 5 pounds of coal."

Working full time Moran can make only ten or, at the most, twelve Damascus blades a year. At present he has orders for the next eight years and doubts if he will even be able to fill those. For that reason Moran accepts no deposits. His top knife, a Viking dagger, is priced at $2,000. The handle of this beauty is crafted of curly maple and decorated with Damascus steel, the sheath has wooden liners covered with fine leather and mounted with Damascus at the throat and tip. With the success of these rare and unusual blades other craftsmen are trying their hands, but the Dean of Damascus is still Bill Moran. Working for many years hammering and forging, Moran finally recreated the lost art of Damascus steel. Other bladesmiths now working in this difficult medium are Bill Bagwell of Vivian, Louisiana, and Don Hastings of Palestine, Texas. A young neighbor of Moran's, who prefers to be called simply Sheldon, is doing some exceptionally fine work at slightly more modest prices, and a blacksmith from Illinois by the name of Daryl Meier is not only teaching Damascus but is turning out fine work himself. In fact, a recent student of Meier was Dan Dennehy, long a blacksmith himself, who has been taught the intricate techniques of Damascus. Even with nearly three hundred knife craftsmen in our land today, there are still only a handful known to be crafting these handsome and unusual blades.

With the growing popularity of the smithy's forge, why are so many knifemen still using the stock-removal method of crafting a knife? It is a complicated answer, really. First of all, not everyone lives in an area where the constant ringing of the blacksmith's hammer won't annoy neighbors. More important, forging requires great skill, long experience, a lot of equipment, and a thorough knowledge of steel and what happens to it under varying degrees of temperature. Let's take a quick look at Moran's technique of forging a Damascus blade.

Begin with a bar of iron and a bar of steel; the proportions must be exact and the right type of steel used. These two pieces are welded together in the forge in the same manner as they were centuries ago. The heat must be exact. If the bar is too hot, the steel will be ruined; if not hot enough, the two pieces won't fuse properly. If everything is done right, the bar is folded and again welded. At this stage there are four layers and the bar is now roughly 3 inches by 3 inches square. Now the bar must be hammered out to about 6 inches in length and again folded and welded. This process continues until the desired number of layers are reached. Moran has tried everything from 16 to 2,048 layers. The best blades and the most beautiful patterns consist of 512 layers. Should the smith do too many folds, the layers tend to become carbonized all the way through and the craftsman finds himself with a solid bar of carbon steel. To achieve the differing patterns, many and varied techniques must be used at certain stages of forging. The more closely the blade is forged to the finished size, the better it will be. It is possible to take a blade with only a hundred layers, grind off a great deal of what was forged, and make the layers appear finer than they really are. Obviously, this is cheating yourself and not gaining a true finish. Added to that is the fact the eye would not be able to see 500 layers in a 1/4-inch-thick piece of steel, as the layers are only one-half of 0.001 inch thick. The problem with any Damascus blade is the fact the smith never knows if it is perfect or not until it is completely forged, ground, hardened, and polished. If it is not perfect, all that work has been for nought. This abbreviated description will give some understanding of why Damascus knives are so expensive.

With his great expertise, and more than thirty years' experience at the blacksmith's forge, Bill Moran can now control his Damascus patterns so that they may be repeated at will. The four he offers are: the ladder pattern, which indeed does resemble the cross rungs of a ladder; a combination of ladder on the back of the blade and an ocean wave along the cutting edge; a full ocean wave; and one romantically known as the maidenhair pattern, which resembles flowing tresses across the blade.

With his present skill at crafting knives, Moran admits to making his first knife when he was about ten years old. Hammering on files and pieces of steel, he used the crude farm forge to make blades that would hold an edge better than a store-bought blade in those days. The popularity of modern knives came about when the Second World War began and the demand for fighting knives from our forces brought the handful of knifemakers to the fore. Randall, Ruana, Moran, and the late John Ek all began making fighting knives for those serving in the jungle areas of the world. In fact, Ek gave away as many knives as he sold. When the film *The Iron Mistress* came out, the bowie craze started and Moran once filled an order with a 16-inch blade. He says, "The damn thing weighed almost ten pounds. It was a horrible monster, and Lord only knows what the customer wanted it for."

When he began his research on Damascus steel, Moran realized how little had been written on the subject. Even the few metallurgists he contacted offered little hope and less encouragement. When he showed his first Damascus blades at the Knifemakers Guild show in Kansas City in the spring of 1972, they caused great excitement among collectors. The blades he displayed were the result of constant experimenting in his shop—much of it trial and error.

First he found that modern steel won't weld together as easily as old steels. They are too refined for working in a furnace. Added to that was the difficulty in seeing the grain. He tried various acids to bring out the texture, and when he was finished, it still didn't show. Finally, in some despair, he thought that perhaps he was using the wrong steel. When he went from W-2, a mild steel, to O-1, the first blade he made and dipped in acid showed a beautiful pattern. Now with the proper steel he had to continue his experiments with heat-treating. While O-1 welded well, it couldn't be too hot in the furnace, since too much heat would cause it to crumble. Drawing the blade was a problem because there was so little information available on Japanese blades. Finally, Moran, after drawing a couple of blades in oil, decided to make one without drawing and found that it had wonderful flexibility. "The trouble with reading up on the old-time craftsmen who did Damascus is the fact that they were one part right and three parts wrong."

One of the things Bill didn't know was if he should have five layers, eight, or a million. The first knife he made had 100 layers, and the grain looked awfully coarse. The next knife had 2,000 layers, and that one was so fine that it was impossible to see anything. He then went back to a thousand folds, and that wasn't too good; so he decided to split the difference and make another blade with 500 layers. After continuing his work for another year or so, Moran began to think that perhaps a 128-layer blade had some qualities and the only way to get these added qualities was to add another piece of iron. It would add toughness and make the grain more attractive. Now, with a goodly number of Damascus blades under his belt, Moran has finally solved many of the problems of those early years of research.

In Moran's opinion, and in spite of the beauty of Damascus, it won't hold an edge any better than O-1. The main advantage is that Damascus is simply tougher. In olden times it was always used for weapons and still makes a great weapon, since the various parts of the blade may be tempered for different requirements. Moran sees no great advantage in using Damascus for a hunting knife because a sportsman must pay more for the privilege of carrying a Damascus blade. In Moran's words, "The man who pays $20,000 for a Purdy shotgun may find it worthwhile to carry the ultimate blade, but the fellow who goes deer hunting once a year is just throwing his money away."

When working Damascus, Moran says that the more welds made, the more likely a mistake will happen. Discoloration will show on the blade and a bad weld will appear as a crack usually running lengthwise rather than across the blade. When that happens, although the blade may cut satisfactorily, Moran throws it away, because it won't please the customer.

The most important item in forging Damascus or any other steel is having a furnace or forge with a good chimney that will draw well. The hazards of a smoky workshop with sulfur fumes are obvious. The one important accessory is a Tuyere iron, an inverted, hollow pyramid that's used to convey the air from a blower at the bottom of the fire. The fire must be at least 5 or 6 inches deep; otherwise, the smithy will be working on top of the fire in a blast of air that will oxidize the metal away. If an electric blower is used, there must be a gate that will control the flow of air. If a hand blower is used, a gate isn't necessary because the air can be controlled easier. Moran cannot emphasize too strongly how important the gate is, as the flow of air must be controlled to exact degrees.

Second, the coal must be a high-grade metallurgical coal. It must be low in sulfur, certainly not over 1 percent. Moran's coal runs about 1/2 percent and he advises checking with the dealer to get an analysis of any coal before buying it. It must also be known as a "high heat" coal; even what mine it came from is important. Always use soft coal, never hard coal. More advice is never put a piece of iron in a fire that has green coal in it. The coal must always be coked. There are different ways of coking coal, and Moran's method is to build a roaring hot fire, pile the coal up after wetting it, and let it burn. Turn it over to coke it thoroughly and once it is burned, sprinkle water on it to put it out.

To make a Damascus blade, Moran always burns up at least 200 pounds of coal converting it into coke before even starting to work. It will take about 150 pounds of coal to make a 10-inch blade.

It takes about two days to burn the coal down properly; then it must be sorted, removing all the green coal. Once everything is set and the coal has been converted, it is stored in large cans for use.

The best way for the inexperienced blacksmith to check the heat is when a scale begins to form on the metal, indicating there is too much air. The welding fire is, in Moran's words, "tremendously hot and runs somewhere near 3,000°F." One of the many hazards in keeping the fire at the correct temperature is that clinkers will form at the bottom of the fire with the bar of steel just laying atop it and oxidizing. One must constantly keep feeding coke into the fire. Every few

Three blocks of steel that will be drawn out for a Damascus fighting knife. The large rod to the right will be welded to the bars and is for the convenience of the blacksmith. Later, it will be cut off.

A well-laid fire with one bar plus the second being heated.

Steel at the proper forging temperature being cut with the "hot cutter."

minutes the coke must be replenished. Experiments with different types of coke will tell the blacksmith just when clinkers begin to build. When that happens, the fire must be respread evenly and the clinkers removed. Then the fire must be rebuilt evenly. Moran has seldom made more than three welds before clinkers begin to form.

But enough of clinkers and fires. To begin making a piece of Damascus steel, cut a piece of O-1 steel, which has 1/2 percent chromium, about 4 inches long, 1½ inches wide, and 1/2 inch thick. Next take a piece of iron of equal proportions to weld these two together in the fire. Before doing so, however, a long iron handle is welded to the bar of steel, which gives the workman something to hold while working with the fire. The pieces are covered with flux that causes the scale to melt or run. Both pieces are then set in the fire until they become welded together. As they form together they are hammered or drawn on the anvil to about 6 inches. Either a power hammer or a hand-held hammer may be used for this step. The small gate is used to center the hot bar, and then it is cut. Moran cuts it about three-fourths of the way through and places it in the fire again. Then it is bent and hammered closed. All these steps must be done swiftly before the heat drops. Moran estimated that these steps take about six or seven seconds; we checked it with a stopwatch and he was only 1/5 second off. It is again placed in the fire and brought up to welding heat. Once it is brought out, there is only about two seconds to make this weld, so tools and hammer must be available because, at this point, if the steel or hammer is dropped, the whole blade can be ruined.

Most expert smiths don't use optical pyrometers; the heat is judged by eye. Moran says that the best way to explain this is to imagine a bar of butter sitting in the sun. When the surface of the butter begins to shimmer, and just when it begins to melt, that is the proper welding heat. Conversely, if there isn't sufficient

Again, at the proper temperature the piece of steel is folded and drawn out again.

154

The third piece is set against the main bar and will be reheated and then worked rapidly on the Little Giant power hammer. This will pack the steel.

heat, there will be a "cold shut," which means that the weld was closed when it was too cold. It will show as a bad open weld in the blade. Moran insists that the weld must be absolutely flawless. If it isn't, the blade won't be any good. A Damascus blade, made properly, is better than a regular forged blade; if not, it won't be as good. All this is critical and takes a lot of practice to get everything to work just right. One of the great arts of the Japanese bladesmiths was their ability to weld at low temperatures and be extremely swift once the steel was out of the forge.

Once a certain number of welds are made, anywhere from three to eight, Moran adds another piece of mild steel to the blade. This piece is about 1/4 inch thick, 3 inches long, and 1½ inches wide. This is an extremely difficult weld to make and must be done swiftly. Once it is welded, it is then hammered out again to about 6 inches and once again folded. Should the craftsman want to add another piece of O-1 steel into the center of the blade, it is done on the eighth weld. This is a very thin piece, and it is a very tricky technique. Advice? Don't try this until skill has been acquired and there is confident knowledge of heat and steels.

About now the steel must be looked at and a decision made as to the length and width of the completed knife. Moran told me, "It's amazing how small a bar of steel you can begin with and draw it out to a 7-inch blade."

One of the problems with Damascus is that the profile, shape, and thickness must be hammered in, *never* cut out. In fact, the blade should be forged so

The Little Giant power hammer. It will work fast or slow depending on the requirements of the operator.

156

Moran examines the drawn-out piece of steel that will be shaped into a blade.

The curves of the blade are hammered out on the horn of the anvil.

The blade being heated again prior to being quenched in the oil.

closely that there is very little grinding to be done once the forging is completed. Moran's fear is that others might try shortcuts and won't make a perfect blade.

Patterns in Damascus blades can be obtained in various ways. Sometimes, Moran feels, trickery is used rather than skill. The Japanese, who are famed for their blades, only use the ladder pattern and accomplish this by forging the bar of steel before the blade is quite finished. At this stage the bar will be a bit thicker than the completed blade. Small waves are forged in, then ground off. This will leave a slight grain showing in the blade. The effect is one of corrugated cardboard or a wave running down the piece of steel. This wave, however, should never run to the edge of the blade and should stop at least 1/2 inch from the edge. Moran emphasizes that under no circumstances should strips of steel and iron be forged lengthwise to obtain the pattern. Such work would be beneath the dignity of a Japanese swordsmith, and it also makes a weak blade.

Frequently, rosette patterns were used to stamp the pattern onto the hot steel. It doesn't accomplish anything except make the blade decorative and isn't true Damascus.

For the man who is attempting his first Damascus blade, the folds must be absolutely straight in order to control the pattern. This means exact control during the hundreds and sometimes thousands of hammer blows making the blade. An occasional quick glance at the edge of the bar will tell if the layers are straight.

Once the blade is forged, it is annealed. This is done by soaking in the fire overnight. Turn the air off, build up a hot bed of coals, and set the blade in the coals. This will slowly bring the steel down to its maximum softness.

The next step is to grind the blade. Small hammer marks are removed, and if the blade was done correctly, there will be very little grinding. Caution, don't try to grind the Damascus blade on a belt grinder. The steel is too hard and will tear the belt. Moran uses a 2-hp 36-grit emery grinder and rough-grinds it first with the wheel. Then go to the square wheel grinder with an 80-grit belt, always using a new belt for a Damascus blade. Much of the work will be done with the 80 grit; however, the 240 grit is used on the ricasso.

Using a jig, the shoulders of the blade are filed square. Next, take a well-used 240-grit belt on a small grinder and grind up and down the edge of the blade.

After all this, the blade is ready for heat-treating. "The soul of the blade is put in at this point," is the way Moran feels about heat-treating. The careful steps include preparing the fire with a large pile of coke. Moran next fills a pail with oil and sets it next to the forge. A large piece of iron is heated in the forge and then dunked into the pail of oil to bring it to roughly 125°F. Moran's warning at this point: "Don't ever quench in cold oil." Once the coal is hot, rake it out evenly over the bed of the forge and cut off air from the blower. Once the blade is set *onto* the coals, there is a theoretical curve where the blade is getting hotter as the fire is becoming colder. At this point some say that the proper time to quench in the oil is when the blade becomes cherry red. Moran scoffs at this since there is no way for two people to agree on just what a cherry red color is. This is probably one of the greatest misconceptions in forging, since many people have made bad blades going by this rule. For example, cherry red in a dark room won't even look red when the lights are turned on. Conversely, a cherry red in a light room won't be close either. Going by this method it is quite possible to miss the correct temperature (1,400°F) by as much as 1,000 degrees.

After the blade is quenched in the oil, it is removed and taken to the belt grinder for the edge to be ground on.

A rough edge is ground.

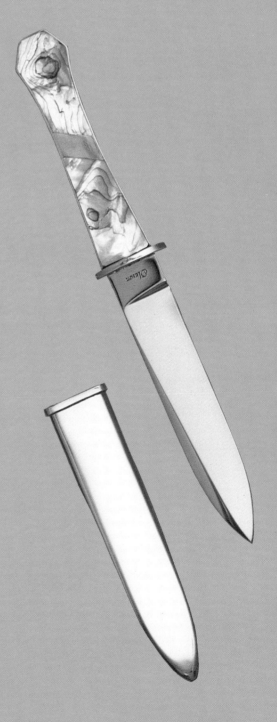

TWO FINE BOOT KNIVES

The knife above, by Ralph Combs, has a superb piece of flaming cocobolo for the handle and sheath. The knife to the right, by Robert Oleson, has inlaid abalone shell for the handle and a silver sheath.

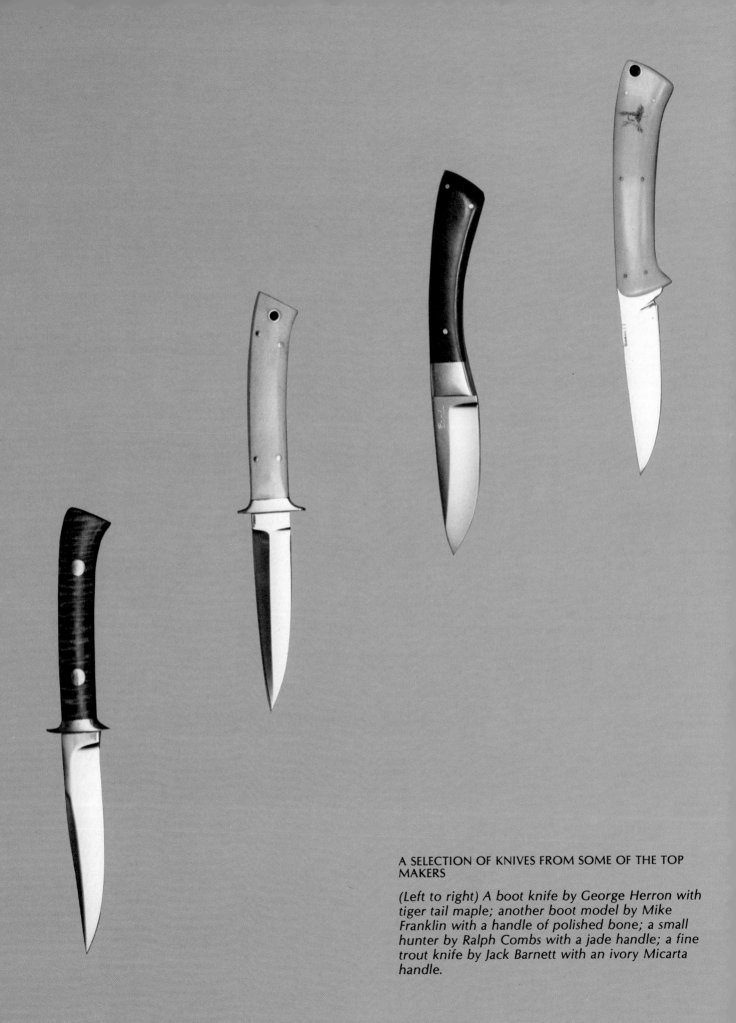

A SELECTION OF KNIVES FROM SOME OF THE TOP MAKERS

(Left to right) A boot knife by George Herron with tiger tail maple; another boot model by Mike Franklin with a handle of polished bone; a small hunter by Ralph Combs with a jade handle; a fine trout knife by Jack Barnett with an ivory Micarta handle.

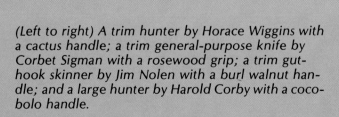

(Left to right) A trim hunter by Horace Wiggins with a cactus handle; a trim general-purpose knife by Corbet Sigman with a rosewood grip; a trim gut-hook skinner by Jim Nolen with a burl walnut handle; and a large hunter by Harold Corby with a coco-bolo handle.

KNIVES FROM MASTER CUTLERS

The two sheath knives are by Ted Dowell and the folder is by Henry Frank. Shaw–Leibowitz have added their striking decor to the blades by etching gold animals on finely detailed backgrounds. Frank is famed for the engraving of his folders. The handle materials are maple and ironwood. The folder has covers of moose horn.

Moran's foolproof technique is to take a magnet and keep touching the blade with the magnet. The exact point at which the steel becomes magnetic is the correct cherry red. This is an easy way to tell the exact time for quenching, and it will work in any shop with any amount of light. Then, right at that instant, quench the blade point first in the oil. Don't move the blade about in the oil, keep it still, since any movement may cause warpage. Incidentally, don't attempt to use motor oil from the crankcase of a car. Special heat-treating oil should be used.

One advantage of a Damascus blade is that it need not be drawn as with other steels. For example, a regular steel blade that wasn't drawn would be useless, since it would be too hard and brittle. However, a Damascus blade may be drawn for extra toughness and it is done in this manner. Remove the blade from the oil at a temperature where the steel is just slightly too hot to hold in the hand. Quickly grind it off on the belt grinder, where the surface is bright and shiny. Then take a blowtorch and go quickly up and down the center of the blade until it becomes a light straw color. Normally, Moran doesn't draw his blades, but lets them sit in the oil until the oil cools down. This will take an hour or two. Next the blade is checked for imperfections by striking it smartly across the anvil. Moran says that this is the quickest way to check a blade, that if it is going to break, it will at this time. At this point, assuming the blade is forged properly, go to the finish grind using an 80-grit belt to grind the edge back on. Next 240 grit, then 500 grit, and finally to the buffer for a finished polish.

After buffing there may be a slight pattern visible, since the buffing wheel may remove some of the softer iron.

To etch the blade, take a large glass container deeper than the blade, and fill it with muriatic acid. The blade is set in the acid and left there for about 1/2 hour. When the blade is removed it is washed in water to completely stop the action of the acid. Baking soda is often used; it is sprinkled on the blade and then the blade is soaked in water to neutralize the acid. The blade is again given a light buff on the machine to remove the dull gray tone left on by the acid. At this point the blade is completely finished: sharp, etched, and polished.

To protect the blade it may be wrapped in tape while the handle, pommel, and guard are put on. As to handles, Moran has been asked if Micarta isn't better than wood. He agrees that it is stronger but also feels that it is not traditional and doesn't, in his opinion, look as good as a fine piece of wood on an expensive knife. The same is true for guard and pommel. Again, he's been asked why not use silver or gold on a high-priced knife? Moran's answer is: "Steel is the medium you are working with, and in my opinion, it's the greatest of all metals. My knives are mounted in steel, and my finest Damascus blades are mounted with Damascus steel for both the guard and pommel." Moran considers this the ultimate, and it's even more costly than silver or gold because the time required runs the cost higher.

The average time needed to complete a Damascus knife is about one month. Remember that another piece of Damascus must be forged just for the mountings, plus the steel fitting on the tip and throat of the sheath.

The fancy sheath Moran slides his knives into is made of spruce, since it contains less acid than other wood. The wood is covered with fine leather, and if it's an elaborate sheath, the throat and tip are decorated with fancy bits of steel.

Oddly enough, Moran has never been able to get an accurate Rockwell reading of his blades. He does know they run somewhere between 62 and 65 and a

The blade is set in a jar of muriatic acid for about 30 minutes to etch the Damascus pattern.

After grinding off the gray smoky scale left by the acid, progress to 240 grit, 500 grit, and finally to the buffer for a finished polish.

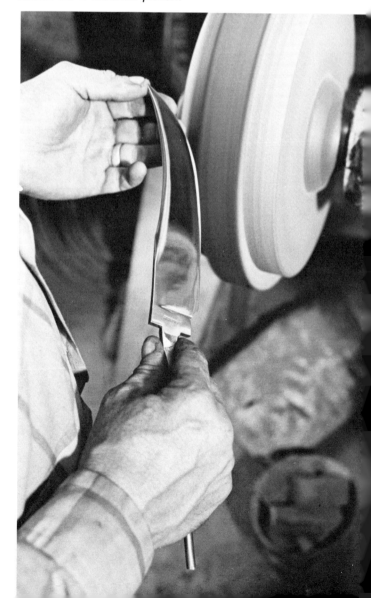

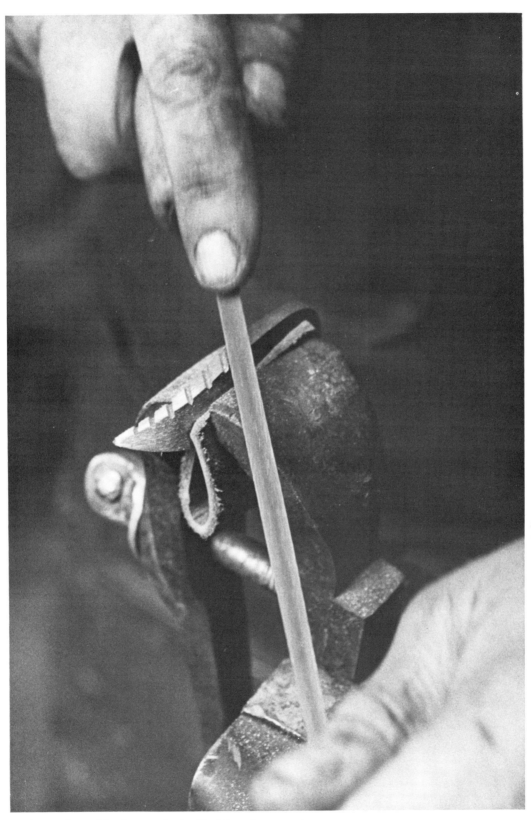

A piece of steel is decoratively filed for the guard.

A block of tiger tail maple is squared off for the tang hole.

After tracing with the handle template, the excess wood is cut on the bandsaw.

Shaping the handle on the 80-grit belt.

Scribing decorative lines into the wood. The gold or silver wire is used to fill these lines.

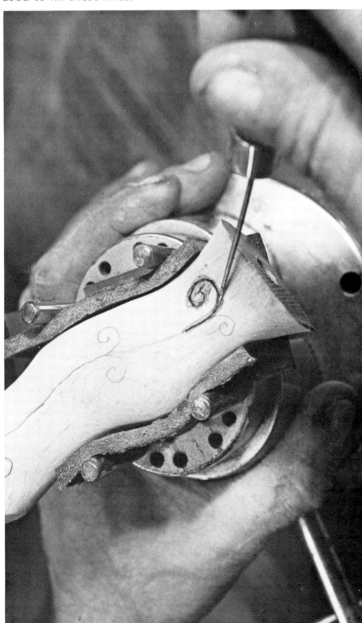

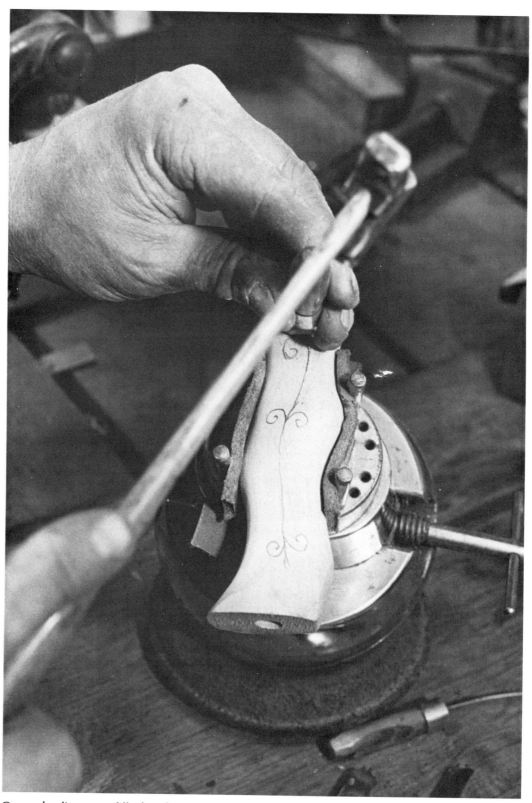

Once the lines are filled with wire, they are tapped down flat using a small piece of steel and a light ball peen hammer.

Once the guard is set onto the tang,
a thread is cut for the takeup nut.

When the nut is tightened firmly,
the tip of the tang is cut off and the
knife is completed.

The finished Damascus fighting knife. The texture of the wooden handle is brought out by applications of a brown water dye. After each application the handle is held over the fire until the heat causes the wood grain to raise. The grain is removed with fine 500-grit sandpaper, and the process is repeated until the wood will take no more dye and the grain stops rising. Once this is done, give the handle a final buffing with a clean wheel.

168

test showed the Rockwell tip going through the soft iron and being stopped by the forged O-1.

To forge highest quality Damascus blades takes great skill and a vast knowledge of both steel and heat ranges. It should certainly not be the first knife attempted by the amateur knifemaker; yet as the craftsman progresses and becomes serious about learning, forging can be one of the most satisfactory methods of making a knife. There is the atavistic feeling that one is working in the style of the ancient armourers, with ancient tools and in the old way.

11 | KNIFE DECOR

Adding anything fancy to a knife may seem as ridiculous as trying to skin an elephant with a razor blade, but decorating a knife with etching or engraving is a matter of personal taste and a man's bank account. A small amount of fine etching may be had for a fairly modest sum. Add gold or silver and the price begins to skyrocket. Now put on a finely detailed bit of scrimshaw in color, some engraving on the butt cap, and quillions, and a fellow could have a nice vacation in Hawaii for what all this would cost.

What impels some men to spend hundreds, sometimes thousands, of dollars to decorate a knife is difficult to answer. It has to lie somewhere between the traditionalists who always favored a little fancy work on a prized Boss or Purdy and the somewhat simpler answer of the man who just wants to personalize a favorite knife. The late Lucian Cary, the great gun writer, once told me, "I like a pretty gun. When the hunting is lousy I can sit on a log and admire the pictures." Perhaps the same might be said of a pretty knife; although it is doubtful if any of these fancy blades will ever sit in a duck blind as the sun comes up or sense the scent of pine along a trout stream.

When the custom knife boom came along a half dozen years ago, most of the highly decorative work was done by the husband and wife team of Sherrill Shaw and Leonard Leibowitz. Acid etching is their forte, and it probably became so popular because steel blades could be decorated either before or after heat-treating. Today there are probably few knifemakers who haven't had their blades touched by the magic of Shaw–Leibowitz with magnificent game scenes, replicas of historic moments, or even a portrait of a favored hunting dog.

Constantly experimenting and improving their skills, both Sherrill and Leonard have discovered the technique of adding gold, silver, or copper to their designs and recently have found a way to add color as well.

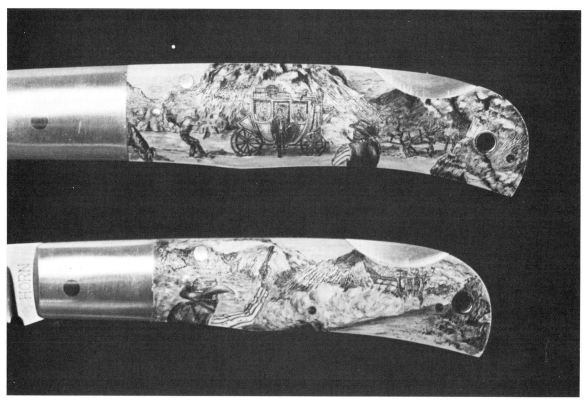

Two folders by Jess Horn with scrimshaw by Michael Collins.

Along with the various methods of combining tones with acid etching are the beautifully painted miniatures of both artists. These are true miniature paintings done on ivory handles that are simply astounding. Sherrill and Leonard claim that because the painting is protected by space-age plastics, it won't be affected by use in the field.

Another popular method of decor is scrimshaw. It, too, has its practitioners of exceptional skill. Michael Collins is a top-flight knifemaker who is equally famed for magnificently detailed scrimshaw in color on ivory handles. A bowie, with the battle of Atlanta in full color on the ivory handle, recently sold for $5,000, which will give the novice knifeman some idea of values in the growing collector's market.

The third accepted method of decorating knives, and probably the most difficult, is relief engraving as done by Henry Frank on his superb folders or the work of Winston Churchill and Lynton McKenzie. The latter two are considered to be among the finest engravers in the world.

Another talented newcomer is Robert Valade, who makes his home at Cove in the eastern part of Oregon. Valade began with guns and has recently been commissioned by Gerber to engrave a series of larger folding knives inlaid with agate. Having worked as a hunting guide for a number of years, Valade frequently marveled at the fancy engraving on guns and knives which his clients carried. In 1968, he bought some engraving tools, and says, "I managed to slip, skid, and gouge out some terrible examples of engraving." He realized that if the quality of his work was to improve, he needed some lessons fast.

Driving to Portland, he spent some time with engraver Rudy Masek, bought some engraving books, and after a few years got a handle on fine engraving.

Valade readily admits to a helpful hand from Colt authority Larry Wilson and Colt's master engraver Leonard Francolini. To date Valade has engraved nearly three hundred Gerber knives, cutting designs into the brass handles. As with most engravers, he finds the hardened steel blades too difficult to engrave and feels the quality of the engraving suffers.

Engraving knife blades is extremely difficult because of the high Rockwell hardness of the blade, and most engravers will work only on the softer metals used in guards, bolsters, and butt caps. Henry Frank, since he crafts his own knives, engraves the blade before it is heat-treated. Even then, Frank admits that the hard steel plays havoc with his tools. Frank is regarded by most knifemen and collectors as an artist without peer for his specialty of elaborately engraved folding knives.

Both Churchill and McKenzie have also worked on knives but are probably more famed as gun engravers and have little time for knives. Even Henry Frank won't take on outside work, although he did a matched pair of knives for Ted Dowell that has been shown at knife shows around the country.

Good engraving or etching is not cheap, and a number of talented craftsmen have learned how to do it themselves. Harvey McBurnette has become a triple-threat-man—he is a skilled knifemaker, fine etcher, and does outstanding scrimshaw. Since Harvey had an art background, all this probably came easier.

Another new name, and a talented artist, is Gene Hooper of Gentryville, Indiana. Hooper, who has been doing scrimshaw for only three years, finds it more rewarding than making knives, which he did for a short time. While many knifemen do their own scrimshaw, since it is easier to learn, few will attempt engraving or etching. Although Hooper admits to help from an illustrator brother, most of his skills were developed from observation of animals on hunting trips and continual practice on white Micarta before even touching expensive ivory.

As to the layman learning scrimshaw, Hooper has this to say: "Anyone can scratch with a needle. How well he does it depends on his artistic skills, how well he knows animal anatomy, and how willing he is to learn." There are two methods of scrimshaw. Mike Collins uses a V-shaped gouger to make tiny cuts in the material. The other method is to use a needlelike tool to make a series of scratches. The latter technique more closely resembles the old seaman's style of scratching the design into the ivory. The instrument may be a needle held in a pin vise, a finely pointed scribe, or any other pointed instrument. And the best advice from both craftsmen is: *don't begin with ivory.*

Hooper, when he was learning, ruined a couple of handles and says: "It's pretty disheartening to work for hours shaping an ivory handle and then practically destroy it in five minute with some careless chicken scratches."

Gene Hooper's method of using needles is perhaps more traditional, since the crews aboard sailing ships used the sail needles for scratching designs into whale's teeth. Collins, on the other hand, prefers the tiny V-gouge that will cut finer lines and, he feels, will make a cleaner cut to accept the colors.

After viewing the skill of these artists it is understandable that fine work can command a hefty price. The selection of a top artisan will also enhance the value of a good knife in years to come. This does not mean, of course, that quality work on a cheap knife will increase in value nor will poor work do anything for an expensive knife. The combination of name maker plus a recognized artisan must

Sheath knives by T. J. Yancy with colorful scrimshaw by his wife, Ann Yancy. The handle material is ivory Micarta.

A matching pair of combat knives by Ted Dowell with engraving by Henry Frank.

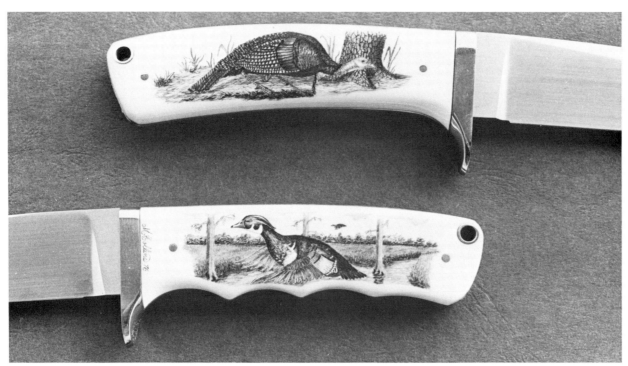

Both knives made by Michael Collins and scrimshawed by him.

An exceptionally ornate knife by Larry Hendricks with etched blade, carved ivory, and gold-engraved and -carved bolsters plus carved gold atop the blade.

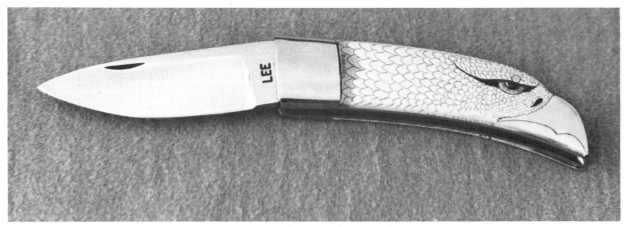

A fine folder by Tommy Lee with scrimshaw work by Don Haynes.

A combined effort by two of the country's masters: the bowie and sheath by Buster Warenski and engraving and scrimshaw by Winston Churchill. The knife sold in 1976 for $6,000.

be combined if the value of a collector's knife is to increase, or at least be maintained.

There is another area of decor that might be called nondecoration—knives so fancy that it would be redundant to add anything to their beauty. A good example of this might be one of Bill Moran's fine Damascus daggers or a classical seventeenth-century stiletto. Another craftsman who finishes his knives in highly ornate style is Lloyd Hale, who does skilled file work on both blade and sheath. And talented Buster Warenski employs silver for sheaths, decorates his knives in exquisite detail, and tops it off with a fancy handle. Knives from craftsmen such as these require no embellishment to make them more valuable or beautiful. Highly decorative knives from quality craftsmen are statements in themselves, and that should be sufficient.

With the growing interest in making knives, talented amateurs might care to try their hand eventually in such decor for their own knives. Let's look at acid etching first. Before going into formulas or techniques, Len Leibowitz hastens to caution the amateur etcher about the hazardous liquids to be used. First, always work in a well-ventilated area, wear safety goggles, and cover your hands with thin surgical gloves. A large pail of fresh water should always be at hand should acid splash onto the skin or clothing.

The knife must be prepared for etching and the handle well taped for protection. All those parts of the blade that won't be etched must be coated with a stop-out liquid. For example, if the left side of the blade is to be etched, the right or opposite side is covered with the stop-out.

Stop-out Formula
4 ounces shellac
8 ounces alcohol
1 gram methyl violet dye

This solution is painted on the blade and allowed to dry for at least fifteen minutes. If the weather is damp or rainy it may take longer. When applying the stop-out, make certain that the edge of the blade receives a heavy coating; otherwise, the acid may eat through the thin coating and damage the edge. The stop-out may also be used to cover the tape on the handle, adding extra protection.

Simply put, acid etching is done as follows:

1. A mixture is used to coat parts of the blade so that they will resist the acid.
2. The design is scribed on the "ground," leaving bare metal exposed to receive the acid.
3. Acid is then applied with a small brush or the blade is dipped into the acid.
4. The blade is left in the acid for a certain amount of time, then removed and the action of the acid stopped by dipping in water.

In telling, the technique appears fairly simple. In the actual doing, it is a little more complicated.

Once the stop-out solution is prepared and applied to the blade, the "ground," or acid-resist formula, is prepared.

Ground Formula
2 ounces Egyptian asphalt
1/2 ounce beeswax
1/2 ounce bastic resin

The mixture is dissolved with either chloroform or ether and put in a small, covered jar. Allow the mixture to settle for 24 hours. Like wine, the sediment will settle to the bottom. Without stirring, gently pour the liquid into another jar. It is now ready for use. (*Caution:* When mixing, have good ventilation and make sure that no one is smoking in the area.)

The method in applying the "ground" is to take a small amount in an eye dropper, then, holding the knife at an angle with a dish underneath, squeeze out a few drops. It should spread evenly over the blade. If there are any uneven spots or high lumps, they may be moved with acetone and done over. (To clarify a little: the stop-out is put on those parts of the blade or guard or butt to protect it from the acid; the "ground" is used to cover the part of the blade that will be etched.) Once the "ground" is dry, and this should take roughly ten minutes, the design is drawn into the "ground" with a fine-pointed instrument.

Acid Formula for Tool Steels
5 parts concentrated nitric acid at 70° F
5 parts water
25 grams silver nitrate

The method of mixing is as follows. The 25 grams of silver nitrate is mixed with the 5 parts of water; then the nitric acid is poured into the water. (*Caution:* Always pour acid into water, *never* water into acid. It could set up a chemical reaction with splashing and sputtering and easily get onto hands or face. When mixing any of these caustic solutions, always have fresh water nearby and mix in a well-ventilated area.)

Stainless steels, because of their high chromium or nickle content, require a different solution for etching.

Stainless Steel Acid-Etch Formula
1 volume concentrated hydrochloric acid, 37 per cent
1 volume concentrated nitric acid, 70 per cent
3 volumes water

Len Leibowitz advises the reader who may encounter a particular stainless steel that won't accept this etch formula to write the manufacturer and request the proper formula for that type of steel.

At this point the drawing is completed in the "ground" and etch formulas are mixed and ready to be applied. The acid may be applied by painting it on with a brush or small feather or by dipping the blade into the acid. Remember that all those areas drawn into the "ground" will receive the action of the acid, while those protected by the stop-out solution won't be affected.

The knife should not remain in the acid too long and, at the start, should be inspected regularly. If the blade is submerged in a clear container, it will be noticed

Leonard Leibowitz prepares a Dowell knife for etching by carefully taping the handle.

The prepared stop-out liquid is first put on the blade and then the "ground" or acid-resist formula is applied with an eye dropper.

When the "ground" is dry, the design is drawn onto the blade with a sharp-pointed instrument.

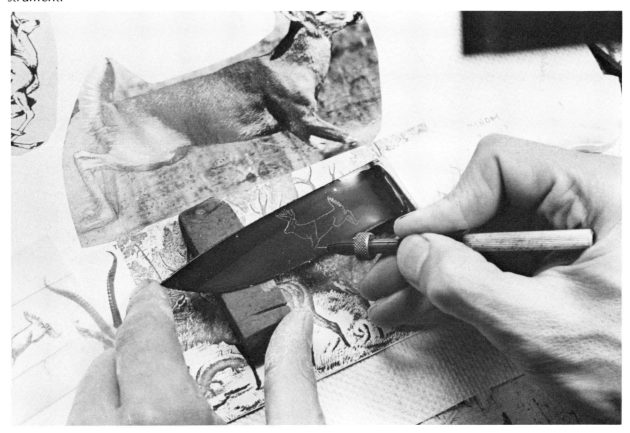

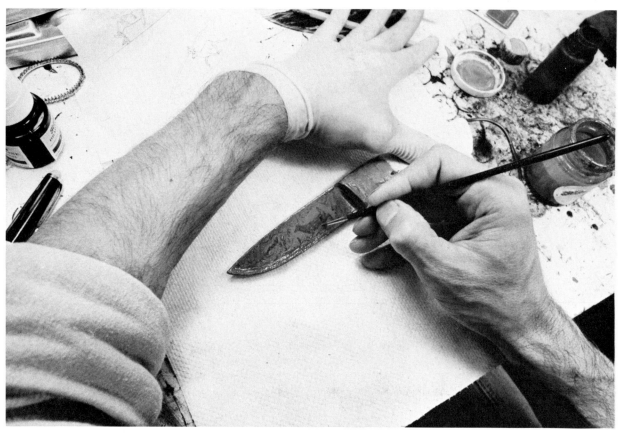

Additional stop-out liquid being painted on to protect certain areas.

As more and more detail is added, various parts are washed off with water for the etcher to gain an overall view of the design.

Len pouring on acid formula to bring out deeper detail in certain areas.

When the acid is finally washed off, the blade is dried with a hot-air blower.

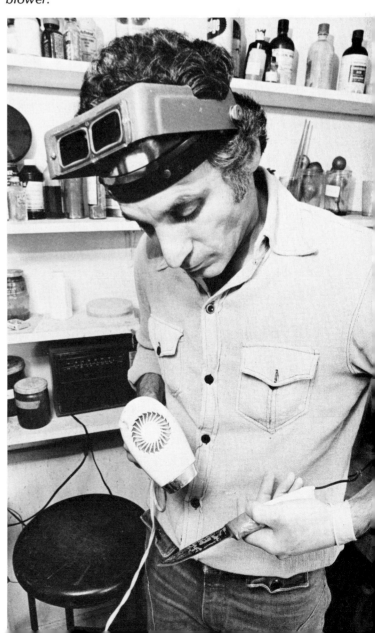

The completed blade is wiped off and made ready for delivery to the customer.

that small bubbles may form as the acid bites into the steel. To obtain clean results, these bubbles should be brushed away so that the acid may continue to bite evenly.

Some cautionary suggestions. If fine lines are drawn too close together, it is possible they will merge if they receive too much acid. This can also happen with fine lines of crosshatching for background or delicate detail on game heads, trees, or leaves.

The acid action may be stopped at any time by removing the blade, washing off with water to stop the acid, and then those areas painted over with stop-out using a small camel's hair brush. Then it's back to the acid. This process is kept up until the craftsman decides that the various lines have bitten deeply enough, all accents are correct, and the overall picture is pleasing. As Leibowitz says, "It's just a matter of biting and stopping, biting and stopping." When the blade has been completed but the etcher decides that some areas are not deep enough, dip a Q-Tip in acetone and clean off areas requiring more acid. Then brush more stop-out over those areas to be protected and immerse in the acid again. With the blade completely etched, the next step is to remove all the "ground" and stop-out varnish. This is done by filling a jar with alcohol and dipping the blade. Take care, however, not to get alcohol on the handle. If the stop-out was used to cover the taped handle it may be softened by an alcohol-soaked cloth to loosen the hard varnish, then cut off with a dull knife. Once the stop-out is removed, the tape can be unwound. The blade is washed with soap and water and thoroughly dried. De-

Sherrill and Leonard examine some of their handiwork.

pending on the skill of the etcher, the result will be a well-crafted knife with some personal decoration that can be admired when the hunting is poor.

Should the craftsman want to gain the effect of gold, silver, or copper, the method becomes slightly more complicated, since the technique is too sophisticated to allow mixing these formulas at home. Of course, if the reader has a solid chemical background, this won't present any problems. For others, however, it will be necessary to locate a supplier who will sell small quantities of the various solutions. In addition, a rectifier must be obtained for changing alternating current into direct current; then both a voltmeter and an amperage meter are required to transfer the various solutions by electrolysis to the metal of the blade. This involves making the piece receiving the metal or silver a cathode; then the anode, usually an insoluble piece of carbon, graphite, stainless steel, or titanium, is put into the solution to be plated. Like heat-treating steel, each solution of gold, silver, or copper has an applied voltage that will allow the metal in the solution to transfer to the plating area.

It is as though the rare metals were being magnetized onto the blade's surface. As with the previous type of etching, it is necessary to stop-out those areas of the blade to be protected. This calls for a special stop-out, usually polyvinyl chloride, that is painted over those parts of the blade for protection. This stop-out lacquer may be obtained from the M & T Chemical Co., Rahway, N.J. 07065. It is called Unichrome No. 323. It might be a good idea to also order Unichrome

Stop-off Thinner No. 3-OP. As the name implies, it may be used to thin the stop-out when needed.

To plate gold or silver it is necessary first to plate with copper or nickle those areas that are to receive the metals. For example, if a jungle scene were etched onto the blade, perhaps a lion or tiger might be covered with gold. In that event, all other areas will be painted with Unichrome 323 to prevent additional acid biting on unwanted portions of the scene. Then the animal can be nickle- or copper-plated, and finally, the gold is put on.

Scrimshaw became popular in the early 1800s when whaling was serious business and then slowly died out after the Civil War. In recent years there has been a growing interest in this old-time art form, and contemporary artists have sprung up all around the country. Modern scrimshaw is now being used to decorate belt buckles, pendants, pistol grips, and the handles of fine knives. Some of this work is done by artists of prodigious talents whose fame can command high prices. Others have been self-taught or at least helped along the way by those of greater skills. One such man is Allen Ford of Smyrna, Georgia. Ford is a knife craftsman of no mean talent and a scrimshander of equal skill who was taught by Michael Collins. Ford's work is amazing for one who has been doing scrimshaw for a short time. In fact, Ford has been known to become upset when his finely detailed scrimshaw is complimented rather than his knives; yet his superb talents are equal in both. On a recent visit to Georgia, Ford showed me a small bowie with an Indian on the ivory handle. At that time he had been doing scrimshaw less than six months. The finely detailed war bonnet and the fringe were delicately shaded in various colors, all blending into a magnificent figure of a Plains Indian in full dress.

Throughout our country great talents are hidden from view (but waiting to be discovered). Some are unknown because their abodes are far off the beaten track, others because they haven't exhibited their work where their skills can be recognized and appreciated. A few don't want publicity at all and are content to do their own thing in their own way.

In contrast, there are those who run their knife business in an efficient manner, go to knife and gun shows, and publicize their talents. One such operation is run by T. J. Yancy and his talented wife, Ann. Yancy once had an automobile dealership in Texas, which probably accounts for the obviously efficient manner of running his knife shop. Ann is a talented scrimshander, having studied art at Southern Methodist University in Dallas. T. J. makes the knives and Ann does the scrimshaw—and fine it is, too. Wildlife themes, animals, birds, and mountains are the most popular. Done in full-color, these handsome miniatures will enhance any knife. While Ann works on her husband's knives, she will also accept commissions from other knifemakers or collectors.

Glen Sterns, of Toledo, Ohio, is another up-and-coming scrimshander who does authentically fashioned work scribed into the handles of knives, grips on guns, belt buckles, and bolo ties. Each piece is one-of-a-kind and is done either in black ink or in full color.

Another fine talent is Gene Hooper, a former knifemaker who turned to scrimshanding three years ago. Unusual for most scrimshanders, Hooper began with white and ivory Micarta, although he finds that the Micartas absorb inks more

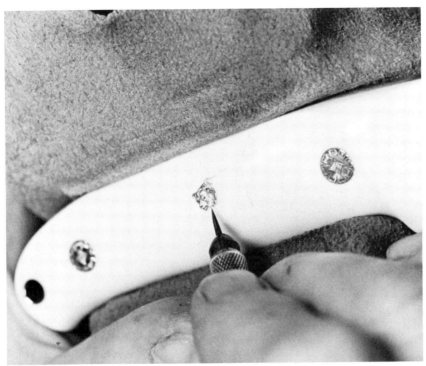

Gene Hooper demonstrates the method of scrimshanding and shows how a scene is slowly and carefully built up on the handle. Out of the picture are a series of rough pencil sketches showing the overall scene. Hopper begins with the central figure of the bear first.

swiftly than ivory. Admitting that his techniques may be a bit unorthodox, he sprays a sealant onto the surface of the area to be worked and then scratches his design in with a small needle held in a pin vise. Once his color is rubbed into a particular area, the sealer is removed with acetone and the area resprayed to protect the finished portion and allow new colors to be put on without running into each other.

For those just learning, Hooper advises Micartas first because any mistakes or errors won't be as costly as tossing a piece of expensive ivory into the trash bin. When the time comes to work on ivory, make certain that it has been prepared properly. The surface may look clean and smooth, but close examination may disclose tiny scratches that are not apparent to the casual observer. In olden days a piece of sharkskin was used to smooth out the surface. The contemporary craftsman has a wide range of sand and emery papers to accomplish the same thing in less time. Start with the roughest paper and then progress through the finer-surfaced materials such as 220 or 400, and finish with a 600-grit paper. Make certain that the surface is really smooth, not just giving a polished appearance.

The tools and accessories required are a small honing stone to keep the needle sharp, a suction vise to hold the knife, and, if your eyes require them, a good pair of magnifying glasses to see the finer detail clearly.

The series of photographs in this chapter show how a scene is built, working slowly and carefully. One of Hooper's tricks is that he blues his needles to cut down on glare or reflections while working.

To begin, Hooper does a number of pencil sketches on paper to get the

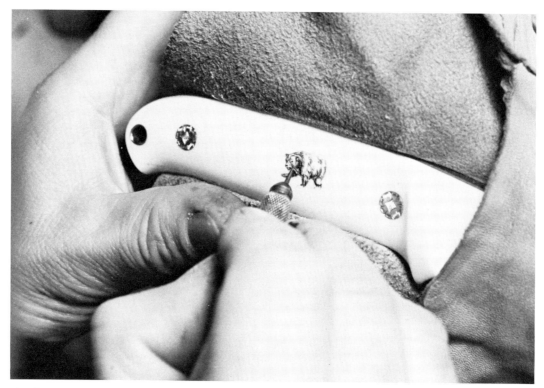

The bear near completion; next . . .

. . . *the background is begun. The bear, plus the background, took about five hours to complete.*

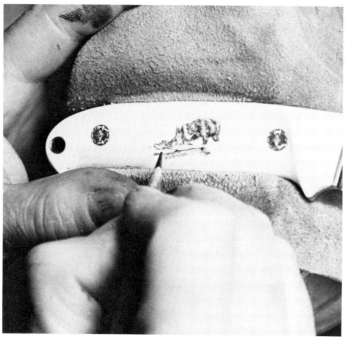

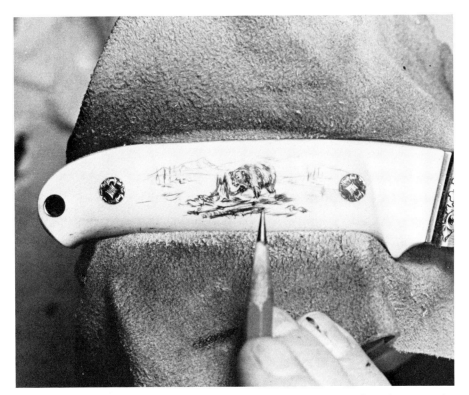

Hooper draws some base areas onto the ivory Micarta with a sharpened pencil.

Hooper sharpens his needle on a whetstone.

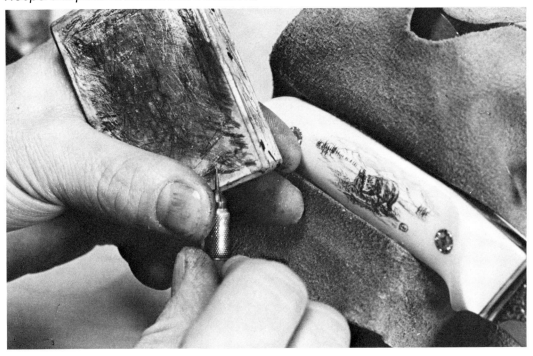

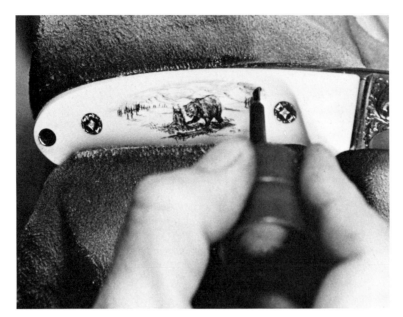

Ink being applied to a mountain for shading.

Gene Hooper working on a knife handle. Note the close-up glasses used for fine detail.

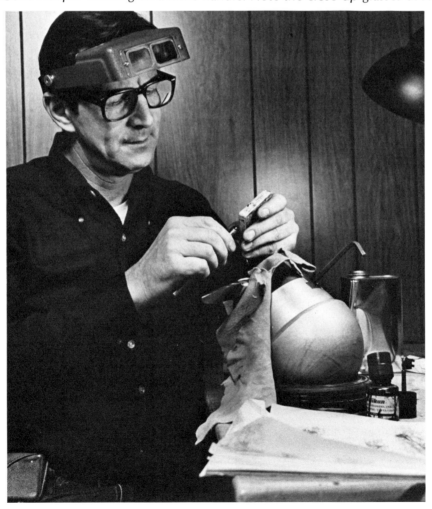

The completed knife with scrimshaw by Hooper and engraving by Lynton McKenzie.

feeling of the particular animal or scene. When he is completely satisfied, he begins work. The sketch isn't transferred to the handle, only used as a guide for the work.

While the scene done on the knife is fairly detailed, the beginner should work on something less involved.

In the overall picture of decorating knives, scrimshanding is probably less difficult, and certainly less expensive, than attempting relief engraving or etching. Those who have the skills to undertake etching will find that it can be a very rewarding method of adding decor to a blade. And a well-etched blade with scrimshaw on the handle can be a worthwhile addition to any knife collection.

12

SHEATH MAKING

Once a knife has been completed, the next step is to fashion some type of sheath to carry it comfortably and protect both the wearer and blade. Although most custom cutlers offer some type of sheath with their knives, not many are enamored of leather work. In truth, most knife craftsmen have told me they resent the time it takes them away from knifemaking, and a couple have grumbled that they are knifemakers, not leather workers. In spite of their understandable resentment, many knifemakers do offer some excellent sheaths, and this is a compliment to both their skill and integrity. Dan Dennehy is known for his top-quality sheaths, and Corbet Sigman delivers careful craftsmanship to complement his fine knives. There are any number of excellent leather workers among the knifemen, but if pressed, with few exceptions most would admit to not liking leather work.

The majority of sheaths made in this country are crafted of leather. In fact, it is the material of choice in making a knife sheath. In the early days, sterling silver was used by Michael Price and Will & Finck of San Francisco to carry their handsome daggers and dirks. Knives, in those days, were worn both with full dress and tucked into a belt when heading for rough country. One modern knifemaker, Bob Oleson of Petaluma, California, emulates the old-time craftsman and delivers handsome knives with abalone shell handles and nickle silver sheaths that could easily pass for the work of those bygone masters.

Other than special knives that are worn on various parts of the body for concealment and require tricky sheaths, none of these are practical for sportsmen.

Probably the most sensible location for any outdoorsman's knife is just aft of the right hipbone. This will make it available for convenient use, keep it away from the stomach should a fall occur, and prevent the wearer from being poked in a soft spot every time he squats down to put another log on the fire.

A variety of knife sheaths crafted by Jack Barnett.

Two sheaths by Bob Heidell following Barnett patterns.

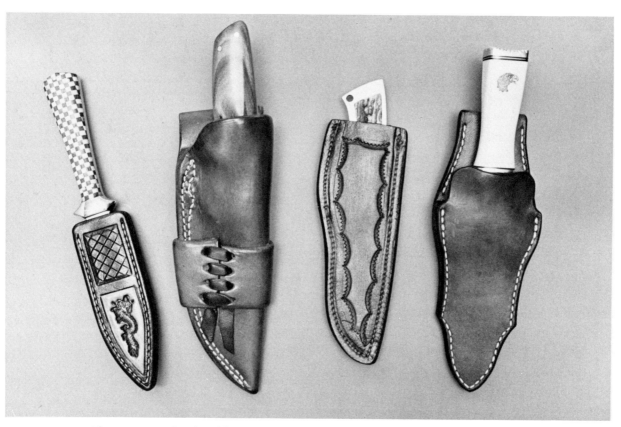

The range and style of knife sheaths. (Left to right) A boot knife sheath by Norm Levine of Dragon Knives; a husky sheath by Jesse Smith; a fine pouch sheath by knifemaker Bernie Sparks; and another boot-knife style by Jack Barnett.

In general, a sheath should be made for the knife it will carry, and it makes sense not to attempt to marry the wrong knife to the wrong sheath.

As with knife styles, there are various opinions, some pretty strong, as to the best type of scabbard to house a knife. Various keeper straps, thongs, or snaps will delight many; while others feel that a well-fitted sheath without extras is the only way to ensure the safety of a knife and make it available when needed. The pouch-type sheath has gained in popularity during the past few years and, in fact, has much to recommend it. A well-made pouch sheath, wet-formed to the knife, will hold it securely and permit the knife to be withdrawn with two fingers. Some prefer a modified 45° angle, much in the manner of the FBI gun holster, and this is accomplished by placing the belt loop at the proper angle.

But before deciding on a sheath, the user must consider his priorities in the field. If he intends to use a backpack or tote a rifle, the various slings and straps may get in the way and cause some problems. On the other hand, a rifle slung on the left shoulder and a knife on the right hip is pretty practical. Even the handgun hunter can usually place his knife aft of a holstered gun without either crowding the other.

As to crafting a sheath, what's required? Some men can do skillful leather work with a minimum of tools: sharp knife, stitching awl, and a couple of sheets of paper for the design. Others, who have had some experience in leather work, will have well-stocked leather shops with an assortment of tools at hand for every task.

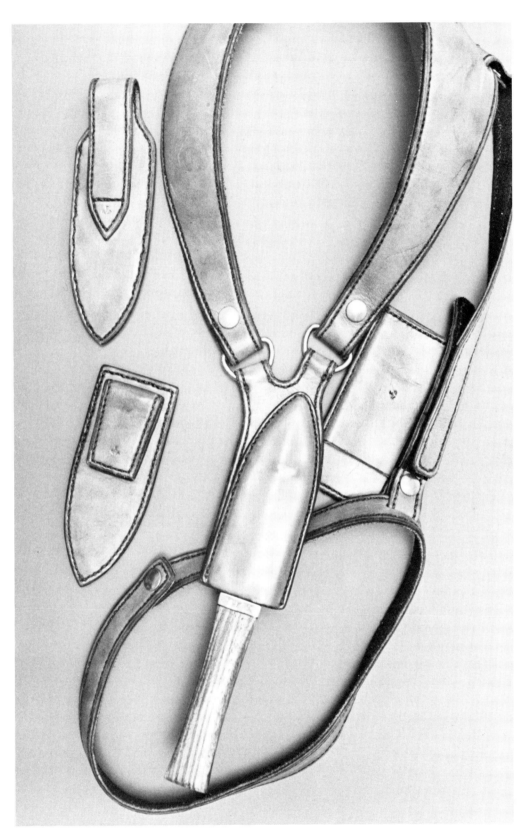

A shoulder rig for a boot knife, with various Velcro-fastened sheaths, for belt, boot, or shoulder. The sheath is by Craig Floyd.

One of the top knifemakers in our country, and a man who admits to really enjoying leather, is Jack Barnett of Littleton, Colorado. While Jack has an admitted love affair with knives, interestingly enough, he has been crafting sheaths for a longer time. Jack feels that a good knife is deserving of the finest sheath a person can make, and his attitude is opposite to other knifemen, for he says: "I love leather work and find it as interesting and fascinating as making knives."

Obviously others feel the same way about his talent, because Barnett is frequently deluged with sheath orders from other knifemakers and collectors.

The first time Barnett attempted to make a sheath was during a sojourn with the navy in the South Pacific, using supplies liberated from the sail locker. Since that time he has given much thought to the making of practical sheaths.

Barnett's advice is to make the sheath of the finest quality leather obtainable. It should be vegetable-tanned since it will wet-form to the knife better. A weight of about 8/10 ounce offers the best protection. Jack's advice: "In making a knife sheath, keep the design as clean and simple as possible. Eliminate moving parts or trick methods of retention and the knife and sheath will offer less problems in use."

As with his knifemaking, Barnett's technique of sheath-making may also be considered unorthodox. For example, he hand-stitches with nylon thread after drilling his stitch holes, uses no rivets, puts in a small brass-lined drain hole in the bottom of the sheath should the sportsman take a tumble in a stream, and even sets a small brass-lined hole in the belt loop for use in hanging the sheath in a gun cabinet. Many regard these touches as a plus, and they certainly enhance the workmanship for aficionados.

The most important part of sheath-making is to make a pattern that will be suitable for the knife to be carried. The leather used for the sheath shown in this chapter is 8½-ounce vegetable-tanned cowhide. Although it may be considered heavy leather, it is entirely suitable for an outdoor knife.

To make a pattern, lay the knife on a piece of paper and outline the blade with a pencil. The craftsman must be extremely careful with the pattern since it is important to obtain the correct fit. Remove the knife from the paper and allow ¼ inch all around for the stitch and welt lines. Fold the paper over as shown, and then cut it out. Use dividers to mark the stitch line about 3/16 inch from the edge; then mark the stitch holes about 3/16 inch apart. All these lines and holes are marked on the paper, not on the leather. Next, the belt-loop pattern is made on paper. Now moisten the leather. This is the time for a word of caution. Once leather is wet, use extreme care with tools and fingers, because any indention on the leather's surface cannot be removed. Once the leather is moist (this can be done using a sponge), lay the pattern over the leather and transfer the pattern to the leather. Bear in mind that this is the pattern only and holes are not to be made in the leather at this time. A scribe, ballpoint pen, or sharp pencil may be used for marking. With the leather slightly dampened, the pattern will transfer easily. Once the transfer is complete, remove the pattern and cut the leather to shape.

The next step is to use a 5/64-inch drill bit to drill the stitch holes; this method makes a neat hole for stitching. The welt must also be cut at this time. After the stitch holes are drilled, the top of the sheath or throat is beveled or edge-slicked. The stitch line is also slightly indented along the row of stitch holes so that the thread, when sewn, lies neatly against the surface of the leather. The type

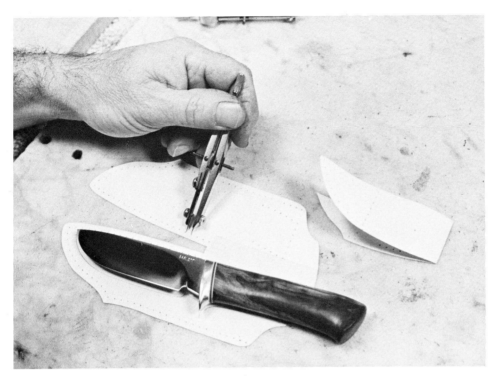

All-leather projects are best begun with a paper pattern cutout.

The pattern is transferred to the leather. Stitch holes have been marked with dividers.

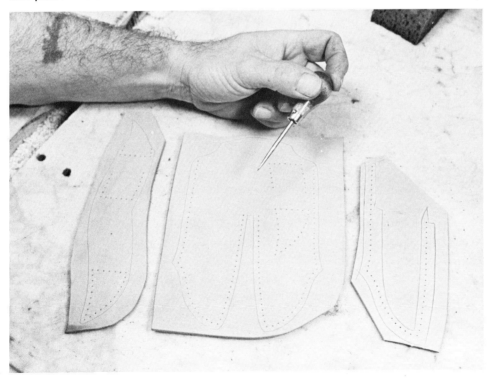

When the stitch holes are drilled with a drill press, a groover is used to indent the thread lines so that a snug, flat stitch line will be assured.

of belt loop shown in the illustration, known as a scab loop, has the end of the loop skived down for a smooth fit. The stitch line on the inside of the sheath must be prepared so that the thread lies flat and won't be cut by the knife when it is placed in the sheath. Now, before any more work is done, take the pieces and fit them around the knife to ensure proper fit. The knife should not jiggle around in the sheath; if it does, it indicates poor workmanship. Assuming that everything is in order, the small brass-lined loop is now stitched on. Barnett's method of doing this ensures that the finished sheath will ride close to the body without any play or movement.

With the loop on, and before the sheath is sewn, the leather should be dyed or stained. Barnett uses Tandy's Maple Tone stain, which enhances the natural finish of the leather. It is applied by pouring a small amount on a rag and rubbing it into the leather. The stain should be allowed to dry at least an hour or two before doing any other work. If a drain hole is desired, now is the time to put it on. The sheath is now ready for stitching. Pull out a sufficient length of nylon thread to eliminate any splices in the middle of stitching. Two needles are used, and each stitch is pulled up tight before going on to the next stitch hole. When the stitching is completed, run the thread back four holes from the end and cut it off. A light flame is applied to the loose ends to singe the nylon and lock it inside the stitch hole.

When the stitching is complete, dampen the leather once again and place

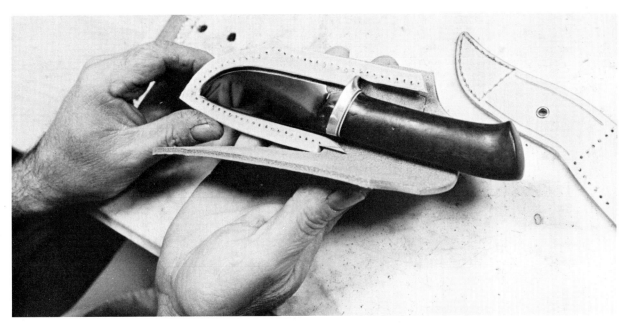

The various pieces of leather are checked for a perfect fit.

A groover is used to mark the stitch lines.

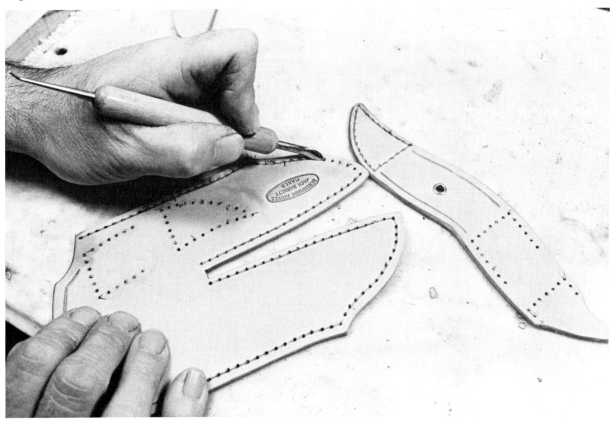

A head knife is used to skive down the edge of the belt loop. This will ensure a smooth, neat fit.

An edge slicker smoothing out the edges.

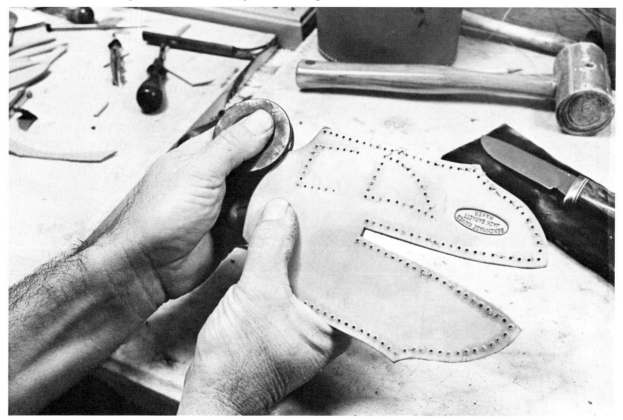

Rounding of the edges with an edge-trimming tool.

Before assembly or stitching, the leather is toned with Tandy's Maple Tone stain.

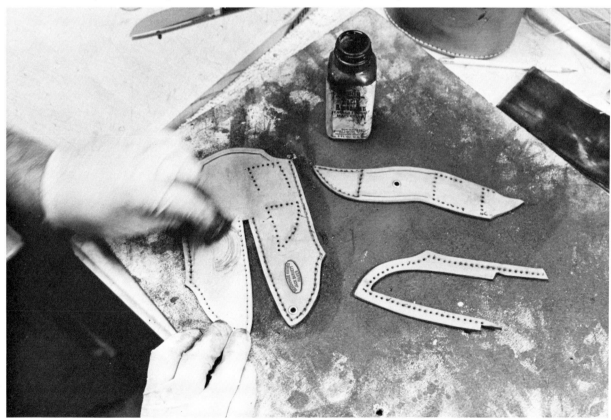

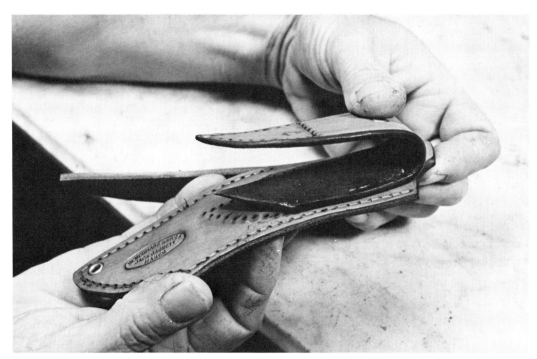

The belt loop is folded before stitching.

Barnett uses two needles, and each stitch is pulled up tightly.

When the stitching is complete, the stitch is brought back for three or four holes; then a flame is applied that will burn the nylon thread into a finished end.

When the stitching is finished, a sharp knife is used to cut away the excess leather.

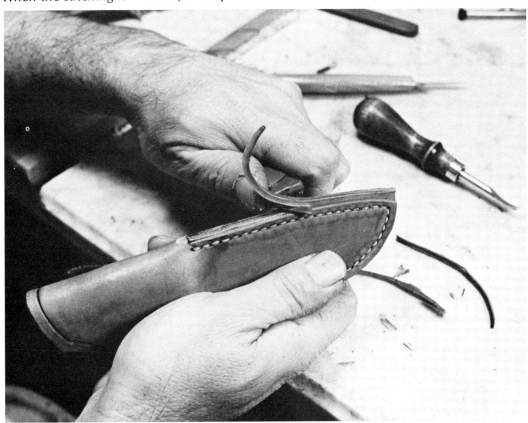

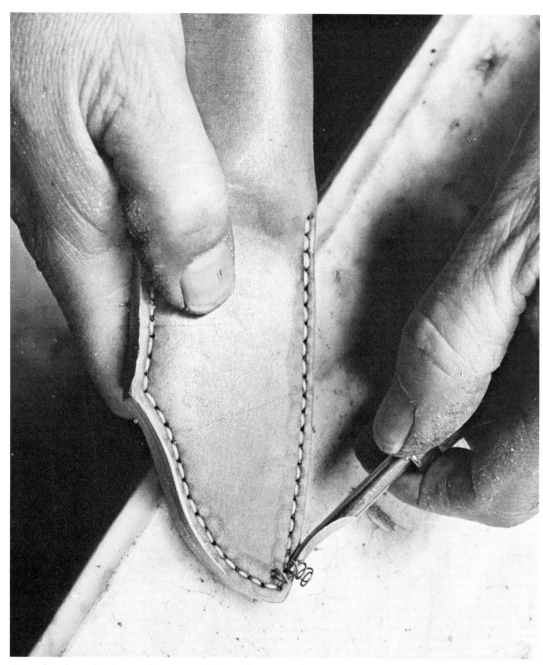

An edge beveler is used to round the edges neatly.

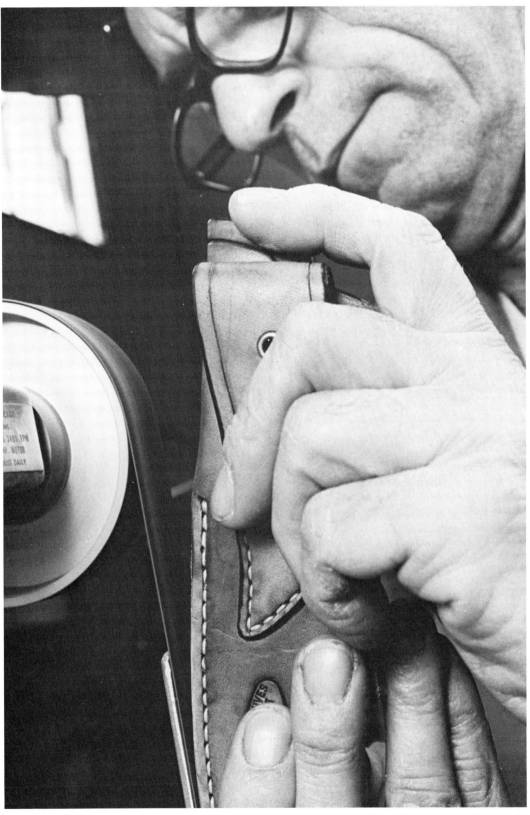

The edges are sanded to remove rough or uneven spots. Hand-sanding will work as well.

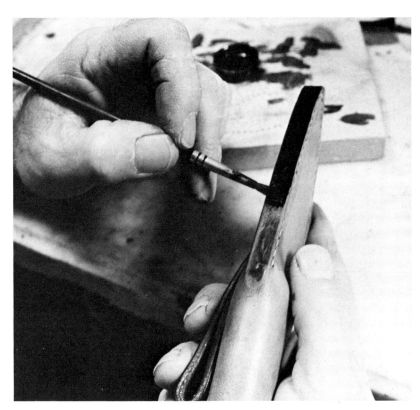

A slightly darker dye may be applied to the edges for a more professional-looking finish.

the knife in the sheath. Form-fit and mold the leather with firm finger pressure, remove the knife, and allow the sheath to dry naturally overnight.

The next morning trim the edges with a sharp knife; then use 120-grit paper to smooth down the edges. Next, sand with a 600-grit paper and slick the edges with an edge slicker. If desired, the edges of the sheath may be stained with a slightly darker dye.

Now comes what Barnett calls his "World-Famous Secret Wax Formula," which is nothing more than breaking some chunks of paraffin into a can, melting it, and then pouring in a bit of saddle oil, which is a mixture of lanolin and silicon. This mixture is heated to a molten stage and brushed onto and into the sheath. Incidentally, numerous applications are better than one since they allow the mixture to permeate the leather. Once a couple of coatings have been applied, the sheath is placed in an oven with the temperature set at 170° F for about twenty minutes. Exercise care, as this mixture can be flammable. This wax finish, combined with the Maple Tone stain, will darken the sheath slightly, giving a most pleasant appearance. After the sheath is removed from the oven and allowed to cool to room temperature, give a coating of Meltonian Saddle Wax and rub it in with a piece of toweling. This will give a finish to the sheath that will be impervious to climatic changes for years to come. Should the sheath become scratched in use, a coating of Meltonian will bring it back to its original appearance.

Incidentally, should the craftsmen prefer a bit of tooling, the time to do it is before the sheath is assembled. Hobby shops have a full range of leather patterns and tools to enable the home craftsman to select a pattern and place it on the leather with ease.

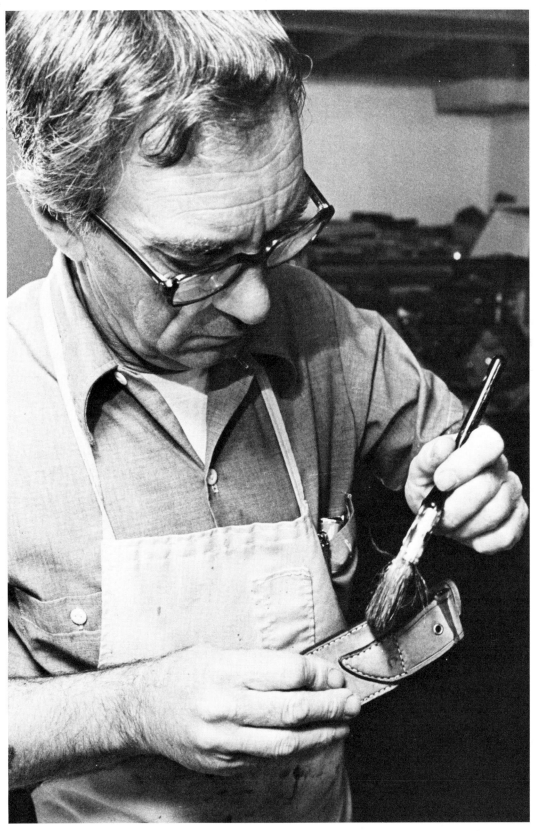

The sheath is coated with a mixture of hot and molten paraffin and saddle oil for protection.

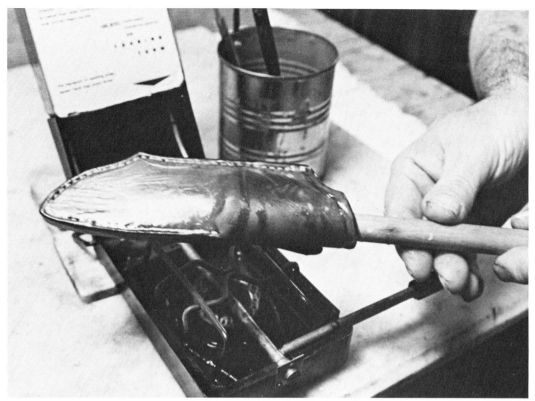

In the final step, the sheath is set over a hot flame at 170°F for 15 minutes; then it is set aside to cool at room temperature.

Jack Barnett admires his handiwork, a well-crafted knife sheath that will work well for almost any knife.

Jack Barnett doesn't claim that these are the only types of sheaths to make, but he does feel they are best for the style of knife he crafts. Barnett prefers the convenience of a pouch sheath without any dangling straps or thongs catching on branches or bushs when in the field. For other types of knives—upcurved blades of skinners or double guards found on fighting or boot knives—another style of sheath may have to be used. however, the patterns, stitching, and everything shown here may be adapted, and as Barnett says: "If the first sheath doesn't fit properly, make another. By the law of averages, eventually you'll make one that's just right."

Many knifemakers have teamed up with a leather worker, either a professional or a highly skilled amateur, to craft sheaths for their particular knives. One such craftsman is knifemaker Sid Birt of Bunker Hill, Indiana. Birt's sheath maker is Craig Floyd, a young man of tremendous talent. Since so many of Birt's knives are combat-oriented, Floyd tends toward concealment sheaths, including some practical shoulder hideout rigs. Floyd also crafts some superb silver sheaths, many inlaid with turquoise, coral, and Indian-type decorative work.

A number of other knifemen have been so intrigued with this type of work that both Birt and Floyd have consented to build such a sheath for this book. Many of the tools required will be found in most knifemaker's shops. These are C clamps, rubber or leather mallets, a jeweler's saw, two steel forms (these will have to be cut out), a wooden punch, a fine metal file, and a piece of 0.040 German silver sheet. This should be at least 4 inches by 5 inches, but make certain that the piece is large enough before beginning work.

The inside and outside forms should be the thickness of the finished sheath minus a thickness of silver times two (0.08), or approximately 3/8 inch. The forms should also be filed exactly to shape, and again, the inside of the forms will be 0.08 thinner than the finished sheath. The outside form, made of mild steel, is roughly 3/16 inch thick and its shape is the same as the inside piece.

To begin, place the sheet silver in a vise and cut in half with the jeweler's saw. Mark the outline of the forms with a pencil onto the silver. Next, anneal the silver before starting to form it. This may be done with a hand-held propane torch. Using small pliers, bring one piece of the silver sheet to a cherry red color, then quench in water. To make things easier while working, the inside form should be marked as to side 1 and side 2. Place the silver sheet between the two forms and clamp in place tightly. Both forms *must* be aligned *perfectly*. Now take a 1-pound rubber mallet and begin forming a sheet around the inside form. This should be done gradually, being very careful not to wrinkle or pucker the sheet silver. Now, being extremely careful not to move either the sheet silver or the two forms, reverse the C clamps and begin forming the other side of the sheath. There may be times when either a wooden or a steel hammer may be necessary to help with forming. Incidentally, it is necessary to keep silver soft and workable; failure to keep silver annealed will result in fractures and wrinkles. After each annealing process the silver sheet and both forms must be returned to exactly the same positions. When forming the bottom end of the sheath, work with a steel hammer. It's been found that medium-soft, glancing blows produce the best results. A small "V" cut is made in the tip with a jeweler's saw to allow further drawing of the metal. Floyd says: "The importance of annealing cannot be overstressed. The silver must be kept soft in order to work it properly."

Any excess silver may be removed from the bottom of the sheath; then place

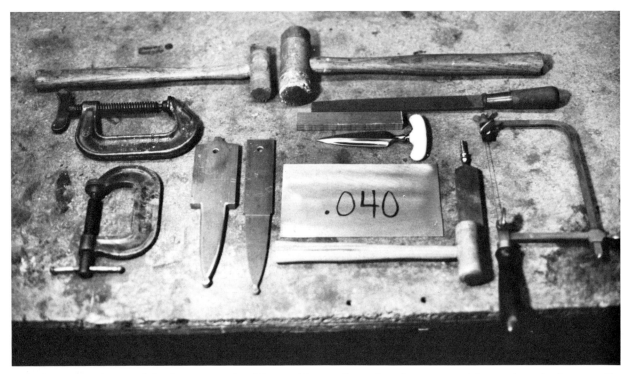

Some of the items required for making a silver sheath: two steel forms, jeweler's saw, rubber and leather mallets, various clamps, metal files, and a sheet of 3/8-inch silver.

Forms 1 and 2 shown with the completed push dagger. The inside form should be the thickness of the silver; it will be roughly 0.08 inch thinner than the finished sheath.

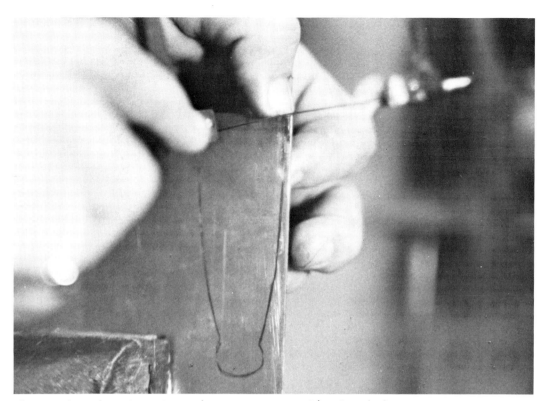

Place a silver sheet in a vise and cut out square with a jeweler's saw.

Checking the size of the silver sheet against the form.

Annealing the silver sheet before starting any forming. Small pliers are used to draw away any excess heat. Bring the piece of silver to a cherry red color; then quench in water.

The inside form should be marked side 1 and side 2. Place a silver sheet between the two forms and . . .

. . . place in the vise and align perfectly.

Using a 1-pound rubber mallet, start forming the sheet around the inside form. Form gradually and be very careful not to wrinkle or pucker the sheet silver.

There may be occasions when a wooden stick may be used in the forming, and this may be hit with a rubber or ball peen hammer. The wooden stick is used extensively in forming the upper corners of the sheath.

Cutting a small V out of the bottom.

Using an X-acto knife to scrape the edges clean.

the silver and the form back in the vise and continue glancing blows while shaping. The wooden punch comes into play and is used extensively to finish both the bottom and top, to form the upper corners. When filing away excess silver, care should also be taken not to remove too much.

Once one side of the sheath has neared completion, the inside form is turned over and the second half of the sheath is made. All edges are filed smooth, and an X-acto knife may be used to scrape the inside edges clean. A background light is used to check the fit of both sides. Hand-filing may be necessary to gain a precise fit, plus sanding to clean the area and surfaces before soldering.

The next step is to wire-wrap both sides firmly together before fluxing. Both Birt and Floyd stress the fact that it is important to apply enough flux, saying, "Better too much flux than too little." Now play a flame over the edges of the sheath to bring the silver up to heat prior to applying the "hard" silver solder.

The flame is applied to the inside of the sheath to draw the solder in. Once the soldering is complete, allow the sheath to cool naturally to room temperature and remove the wire.

It is suggested that a wire brush be used to remove hardened flux to prevent clogging of files. Gently place the sheath in a leather-padded vise and use both files and sandpaper for final shaping. Once this is done, the silver sheath is polished with 240-grit polish; then the throat or turned area of the push dagger will determine the location for the top cut on the sheath. This area is marked, and

Hand-filing for a precise fit.

Using a backlight to check for perfect fit of the two sides.

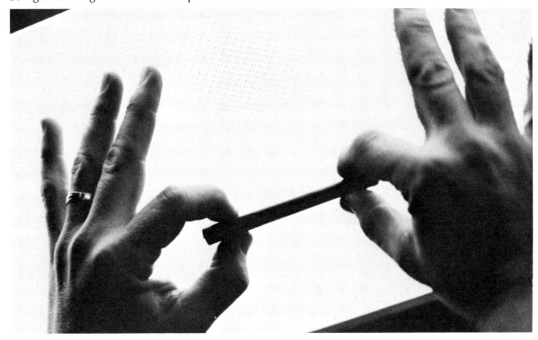

Using safety wire, wrap both sides of the sheath firmly together. The sheath is now ready for the soldering flux.

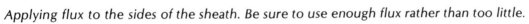

Applying flux to the sides of the sheath. Be sure to use enough flux rather than too little.

Playing a flame over the sheath to bring the silver up to heat prior to applying hard silver solder.

Using a wire brush to remove hardened flux.

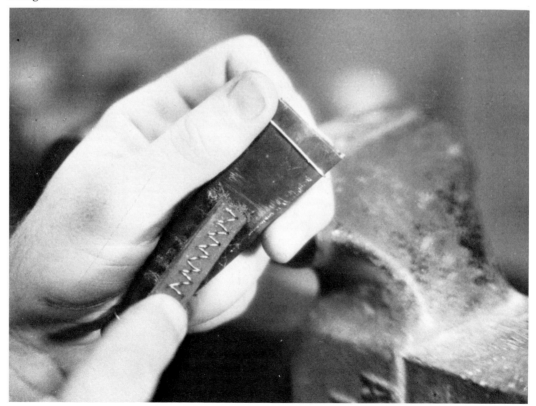

Once the sheath is placed between two pieces of leather in a vise for removal of excess solder, it is polished with a 240-grit polish.

any excess silver will be cut or filed away. A half-round file is used to shape this section. Another piece of German silver, 0.040 thick, is now marked and rough-cut to shape. This piece will form the top cover of the sheath and its attaching clip.

The top of the inside form is now used to shape the top cover. Before shaping, anneal only the area that will cover the top; *do not* anneal the attaching clip. Shape the top cover using a rubber mallet and ball peen hammer. Check frequently for fit as the work progresses. A hole is drilled before soldering to allow gas to escape and permit filing of the entry slot. After cleaning all edges to be soldered, apply flux, and solder the top cover to the sheath. The next step is to file, sand, and polish (240-grit polish) all inside edges. This must be done *before* the clip is bent to shape.

Next, go from the 240-grit finish directly to the final polish with Green Chrome. A muslin 10-inch wheel is used at 1,800 rpm; you'll need a lot of paper towels to wipe the sheath often to check the work.

A paper towel is used to wrap the sheath and protect the polish before cutting into the top of the sheath for blade entry. Using various shapes of jeweler's files, the slot is filed to shape. Be sure to remove all burrs inside the slot and, when checking the blade fit, be certain to allow sufficient space to insert velvet lining. Once the final polish is completed, the sheath is completely soaked in scalding water to clean out the inside before epoxying the liner in place.

The throat or turned area of a push dagger will determine the location for the top piece on the sheath.

Another piece of 0.04 German silver is marked, rough-cut, and formed to shape. This will form the top cover of the sheath and its attaching clip.

Once the attaching clip is soldered on and all sections filed and polished to smoothness, plus soaking the entire sheath in scalding water to clean up the inside, a clean push rod is used to coat the inside with epoxy.

Two pieces of linen material, previously cut to size and pushed inside and pressed down. Do both pieces of linen at the same time.

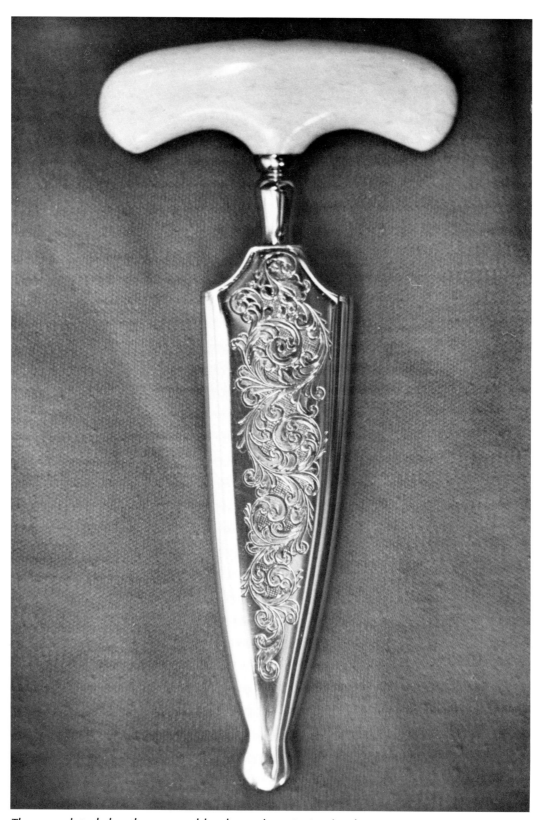

The completed sheath engraved by the maker, Craig Floyd.

The liner is cut to the shape of the outside of the sheath—in two pieces, just as the sheath was made. Using a clean rod, insert and press down on the liner material, doing both pieces at the same time. Once the liner is dry, the sheath is complete. It may be engraved, as the one was that is shown here, or left plain. The time consumed in making the silver sheath was about ten hours.

Other knifemen who have their sheaths crafted for them are Rod Chappel and Roger Russell, both of Spokane, Washington. Jesse W. Smith of Spokane is an experienced saddle maker and leather craftsman who makes superb sheaths for both knifemakers. Only the finest leathers are used, and each sheath is wet-formed to the individual knife. All these makers, including Craig Floyd, accept commissions from other knifemakers and collectors. None of these craftsmen shortchange their customers, and a sheath from any of these artisans is sure to delight and please the recipient.

13 ∥ KNIFE SHARPENING

When a benchmade knife is delivered to the customer, it invariably has a keen edge, placed on the blade by the maker. This is usually the final step in making a custom knife, and if the steel is 154-CM or Stellite 6-K, the new owner will find that the edge remains finger-cutting sharp for quite some time.

However, the day will eventually arrive when that beautiful knife will require resharpening, and that's when a twinge of fear often strikes. In fact, that same fear touches the knifemaker, too, because he doesn't want to see a fine knife ruined by the use of improper sharpening techniques. Granted that putting an edge on a knife demands some skill, the thought needn't send shivers down your spine.

The professional knifeman usually puts the edge on his blades with a grinding belt or, in some cases, by use of a Norton stone cradle, a device that holds three different grit stones in an oil bath. Unfortunately, too many knife users have been brainwashed over the years by watching their neighborhood butcher whisk his knife along a steel and then proceed to cut and trim a piece of meat. There is nothing wrong with this if the sportsman's blade, like the butcher's, happens to be a piece of soft carbon steel, but fine custom knives are crafted of steel that has a high chromium content plus high Rockwell hardness, neither conducive to placing an easy edge on a quality knife.

The secret (and it really isn't a secret) lies in the use of proper tools. This means good-quality honing stones, a cradle to hold the stones firmly when in use, a generous amount of good honing oil, and the ability to hold the blade at the proper angle stroke after stroke. Quality stones aren't cheap, but the man who pays a couple of hundred dollars for a knife, or the fellow who put in sixty hours or

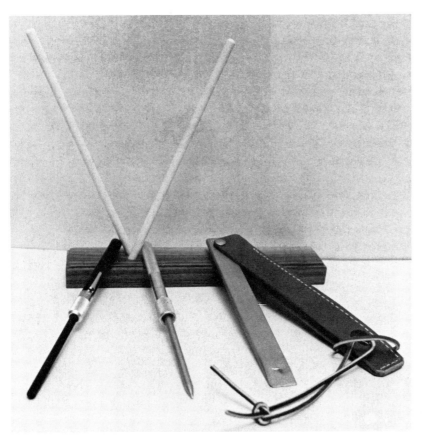

Various aides to keeping an edge on a knife. The two upright rods are A. G. Russell's Crock Stick. The alumina ceramic sharpener does a first-class job of keeping a razor edge on any knife. The black rod is the Buck Edgemaster, which can be worn in the pocket with a pen clip. The Eze-Lap diamond knife sharpener is excellent for all blades, particularly for Stellite blades. The large sharpening steel is by Gerber and has a wedge edge for splitting logs.

more making his own knife, doesn't want to stint on the gear that will allow the knife always to be put in use with a proper edge.

The question of how long a stone to use always arises. The answer is that the stone should be as long as the longest blade owned.

Once the stones are obtained—and two are required, an Arkansas Medium plus an Arkansas Surgical Black, each running 6 to 8 inches long and costing about $30—a stone cradle should be set up to hold the stones firmly with a C clamp and good honing oil. The cradle will run about $4 and the oil another $1.50. Pour a generous amount of oil onto the stone and smear it about with the fingers; then *press down hard* as the blade is drawn across the surface of the stone. Easy swipes will accomplish nothing for the blade and less for the user, except to keep him occupied longer. Granted that such steels as 154-CM or 440-C may take a bit longer, the hard downward pressure is what puts an edge on a knife.

The angle of the edge is of the utmost importance, and the same angle must be sustained for each stroke across the stone. If the new knife owner finds it difficult to maintain this angle, there are a couple of devices on the market that will make the job easier. A few years ago Buck knives introduced the Buck Honemaster.

It clamps onto the blade and fastens with a thumbscrew that holds it firmly in place. The inside of the device, the part that clamps onto the blade, is lined with neoprene and won't mark or scratch the blade. In use, the Honemaster will hold the correct angle, although toward the tip of the knife the handle must be lifted a bit when sharpening. A little practice will ensure the correct method of doing this. A similar instrument is marketed under the name "Razors-Edge." This device fastens with a small Allen wrench. Since there is no protection for the blade, it is suggested that tape be used to cover the blade before clamping down hard. Both work equally well with, perhaps, a slight edge to the Honemaster for ease of placement on the blade.

The oil is important, too, since it will allow the blade to be drawn easily across the stone as well as floating tiny particles of steel to the surface. Everyone usually asks how many times the blade should be taken across the stone. The answer is, of course, as many times as is necessary to place a proper edge, but Andy Russell, the knifemaker from Arkansas, says that a dozen strokes in each direction should ensure a proper edge.

Like everything else, sharpening shouldn't be overdone. An edge that permits shaving won't be much good for anything else. Cutting kindling or fuzz sticks for a fire might easily break off tiny particles of steel and even require that a new bevel be ground onto the blade.

One of the most difficult materials to sharpen is a blade made of Stellite 6-K. It is exceptionally hard and requires something special. Mike Franklin, the leading exponent of this unique material, has found the Eze-Lap rod, with its diamond-impregnated surface, to be probably the best device for keeping an edge on a Stellite blade. Even with this tool, some extra elbow grease may be required.

One of the most innovative and interesting sharpening devices is the LoRay sharpener. I must confess that when I first saw the LoRay, I likened it to a Rube Goldberg invention, with various sections fastened to each other and rods placed in a hole for guidance; but believe it or not, the thing works, and with a bit of patience, it will place a fine edge on any knife from folders to a 10-inch sheath knife.

The LoRay will refinish chipped edges and can place an angle from 17 through 20 and 25°, depending on the hole the guide rod is placed in. The LoRay employs three different grit stones, with the 100-grit being used first, then progressing to the 320-grit medium stone, and finally the 600-grit hard stone, to complete the job. The trick is to work a burr along the edges of the blade with the rough grit, then move in sequence to the finer stones. The LoRay is the exception to heavy pressure; the various stones should be stroked lightly across the edge of the blade. Placing an edge with the LoRay will take patience, but this is the one instrument that maintains the proper angle for the amateur and will put a fine edge on any knife within a short time.

How about those small stones found riding on a sheath? They may be all right for an emergency touch-up in the field, but they are of little value in doing a first-rate sharpening job.

There is no doubt that sharpening a knife properly does require some practice, and before beginning on a quality knife it is a good idea to practice on some inexpensive kitchen knives to attain skill.

The various gut hooks on some knives will require attention, too, if used frequently to zip open an animal. Some men use a small, fine jeweler's file and then

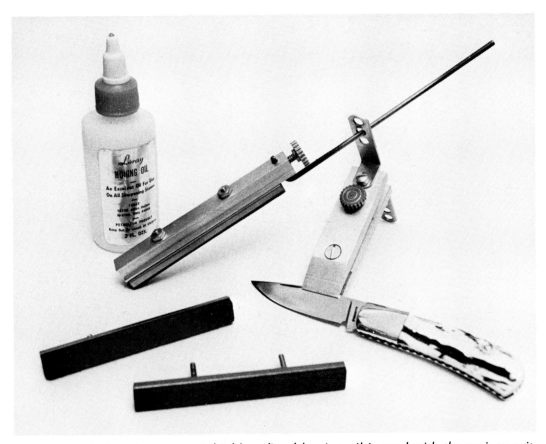

The unique LoRay sharpener. A highly refined honing oil is used with the various grit stones. The guide placed in the proper hole will give various angle degrees to maintain the edge.

finish the job with a small round stone, moving it gently over the inner edges of the hook.

Aside from doing damage to a knife by poor sharpening techniques, the second greatest hazard, and one that makes knife experts cringe, is misuse of the blade. This covers throwing, heavy cutting, opening tin cans, or using the blade as a screwdriver. Earlier we said that a blade is for cutting meat or game. Digging out holes in wood, cutting baling wire, or scraping paint off metal is a sure way to quickly ruin a fine knife.

In spite of what we said earlier about sharpening on a steel, there are some excellent steels available for touching up a blade in the field. These hone steels, made by Gerber and Schrade, will slick up an edge swiftly and keep a blade in fine cutting condition when working on an elk or deer. Remember, however, that these steels are for use in the field and should not be used for putting an original edge on a blade.

Once a knife is sharpened to the user's pleasure, it makes sense to strop or draw it across the palm a couple of times. This will set the edge and, perhaps, bring a look of awe to a chum's face.

The care of a knife when not in use is fairly simple. Once the blade is sharpened, it may be washed off in warm, soapy water and dried. Storing a knife is easy, too. After it's cleaned, put a few drops of oil on the blade, wrap in wax paper, and

The proper angle for moving the blade edge across the stone. Note the roll of oil in front of the blade. A dozen swipes on each side of the blade should be sufficient to put an edge back on a dull knife.

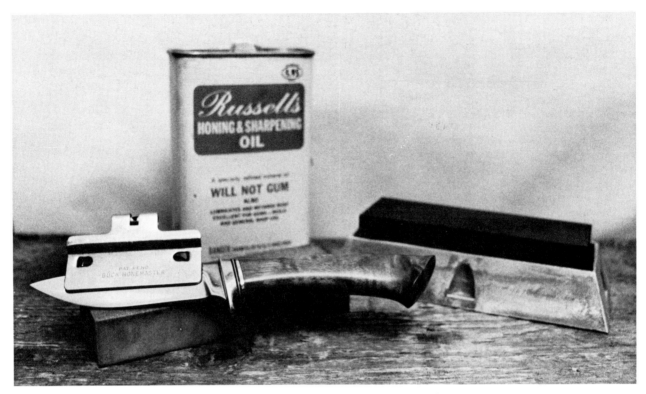

Morseth sharpening stones and the Buck Honemaster, a fine device for helping to maintain the proper angle while sharpening.

place in a drawer. Never, repeat never, store a knife in its sheath, since the tanning acids can set up an action on steel that may rust and pit the blade.

When the stones become dirty, just wash them off in warm water and, if necessary, pour oil on the surface to float the bits of steel up so they may be wiped off. After washing, allow the stone to dry at room temperature; then place it in its box and put it away.

Common sense is the best guideline to protecting a knife. If the knife is used for its intended purpose, it will give its owner long and faithful service.

14

KNIFEMAKERS AND SUPPLIERS

This list of nearly three hundred knifemakers in no way implies approval or disapproval by the author. There are undoubtedly many knifemakers of fine character and reputation who are not listed, plus some who are listed who should, perhaps, not be. As for giving large deposits when ordering knives, that is a matter best left to the buyer's conscience. It is recommended, however, that a minimum of $1 be sent for each catalog requested. Most professional knifemen maintain small, one-man shops, and color catalogs can be expensive items.

Taylor Agee
Rt.1, Box 56
Farmville, VA 23901

John Alexander
72 Jaminska Road
Maple, WI 54854

Lendall Amick
753 Pine Wood Avenue
Hueytown, AL 35020

Ronnie Amick
1445-B Rollingwood
Sylacauga, AL 35150

A. W. Amoureux
2311 Barrow
Anchorage, AK 99503

E. R. Andrews
Box 437
Hazelwood, MO 63042

W. E. Ankram
1260 North Milford Road
Highland, MI 48031

Victor Anselmo
6109 Clybourne
North Hollywood, CA 91606

B. J. Backward
Box 903
Farmington, NM

Bill Bagwell
Box 869
Vivian, LA 71082

Baker Knives
Box 514-B
Hinsdale, IL 60521

Larry Bamford
1712 Carlisle Road
Oklahoma City, OK 73120

Barbee Knives
Box 1702
Fort Stockton, TX 79735

Jack Barnett
1496 East Caley
Littleton, CO 80121

Jack Barrett
2133 Peach Orchard Road
Augusta, GA 30906

Brian Baylis
1390 Orphus Avenue
Leucadia, CA 92024

Beck Knives
1504 Hagood
Barnville, SC 29812

Jack Belk
P.O. Box 252
Kittredge, CO 80457

Benchmark Company
P.O. Box 12121
Rock Hill, SC 29730

Benton's Custom Knives
Rt. 1, Box 395
Ingleside, TX 78362

Les Berryman
7122 Calais Place
Newark, CA 94560

Bill's Custom Knives
R.D. 1, Box 163
Waymart, PA 18472

Sid Birt
P.O. Box 544
Bunker Hill, ID 46914

Bizai Knives
P.O. Box 16555
Raytown, MO 64133

John Black
1225 Evergreen
Richardson, TX 75080

Bone Knives
806 Avenue J
Lubbock, TX 97401

Lew Booth
16 Cypress Terrace
Boonton, NJ 07005

H. G. Bourne
1252 Hope Avenue
Columbus, OH 43212

Francis Boyd
1930 Kern Street
San Francisco, CA 94133

David Boye
Box 87
Davenport, CA 95017

Oran Breeze
11 Oak Park Lane
Bluford, IL 62914

G. M. Britton
Rt. 2, Box 271-B
Kinston, NC 28501

Dennis Brooker
1428 Frazier
Des Moines, IO 50315

D. L. Brown
1803 Birdie Drive
Toledo, OH 43615

Floyd Brown
1940 Southwest 83rd Street
Miami, FL 33155

Lynn Brown
301 East Neece Street
Long Beach, CA 90805

Brown & Pharr
1775 Wilwat Drive
Norcross, GA 30093

Buffalo Jon
Box 474-C
Benson, AZ 85602

John Bugden
106 South 13th Street
Murray, KY 42071

Bill Bullard
Rt. 5, Box 33-d
Andalusia, AL 36420

Ray Busch
940 Orion Avenue
Metaire, LA 70005

Peter Callan, Jr.
7813 River Road
Wagerman, LA 70094

R. C. Campbell
365 West Oxford Avenue
Englewood, CO 80110

Ronald Canter
201 North Hays Avenue
Jackson, TN 38301

Randy Carlson
Box 163
Moscow, ID 83843

Wyndel Carnes
Box 18
Whitesburg, GA 30185

Fred Carter
2303 Dorothy
Wichita Falls, TX 76306

Bill Cassaberry
Box 2005, Castle Park
Valdosta, GA 31601

Frank Centofante
Box 17507
Tampa, FL 33612

Eduardo Chain
13 Avenida Norte N° 12
San Salvador
El Salvador, C. America

Rod Chappel
Davis Custom Knives
North 1405 Ash
Spokane, WA 99201

Chase Custom Knives
P.O. Drawer H
Aledo, TX 76008

Cheatham Knives
2930 West Marlette
Phoenix, AZ 85017

D. E. Clark
Box 216, Woodlawn Street
R.D. 1
Mineral Point, PA 15942

Roger Clark
2624 West Belmont
Phoenix, AZ 85203

J. D. Clay
Box 4A, Graysbranch Road
Lloyd, KY 51156

Dan Cockrell
19845 East Cienega Avenue
Covina, CA 91724

Michael Collins
Rt. 4, Batesville Road
Woodstock, GA 30188

Walter Collins
Box 10311
Rockhill, SC 29730

Ralph Combs
P.O. Box 1371
Naples, FL 33940

John Nelson Cooper
Box 1423
Burbank, CA 91505

Harold Corby
1714 Brandonwood Drive
Johnson City, TN 37601

Joseph Cordova
Rt. 1, Box 1636-A
Albuquerque, NM 87105

David Cosby
1016 Cliff Drive, Apt. 111
Santa Barbara, CA 93101

Don Couchman
Star Route
LaMesa, NM 88044

H. W. Crabtree
Rt. 1
Alama, AR 72921

Mike Craddock
Rt. 1, Box 202-C
Burlington, NC 27215

Craig Knives
334 Novara
Manchester, MO

Crawford Knives
205 North Center
West Memphis, AR 72301

W. W. Cronk
511 Boyd Avenue
Greenfield, ID 46140

John Culpepper
2101 Spencer Avenue
Monroe, LA 71201

Jim Cunningham
1519 Madison
Memphis, TN 38104

Orville Dachtler
35182 Cabral Drive
Fremont, CA 94536

Dagget Knives
Rt. 1
Stewart, OH 45778

Rick Darby
4026 Shelbourne
Youngstown, OH 44511

Stephen Davenport
301 Meyer
Alvin, TX 77511

Davis Bros.
P.O. Box 783
Camden, SC 29020

Davis Knives
1469 East Lexington
El Cajon, CA 92021

Larry Davis
411 Cedar Drive
Pierce, ID 83546

W. C. Davis
Box 96, R.R. 2
Raymore, MO 64083

Phillip Day
Rt. 1, Box 465-T
Bay Minette, AL 36507

Gary Decker
2207 Breenwell
Baton Rouge, LA 70805

DeLeon Knives
1920 East 14th Street
Lubbock, TX 79403

Dan Dennehy
Box 2-F
Del Norte, CO 81132

Julius Diana
P.O. Box 152
Carmichael, PA 15320

Charles Dickey
803 Northeast A Street
Bentonville, AK 72712

Frank Didson
29 Flintwood Drive
Little Rock, AR 72207

Charles Dohogne
Manchester, TN 37355

T. M. Dowell
139 St. Helens Place N.W.
Bend, OR 97701

Robert Dozier
P.O. Box 58
Palmetto, LA 71358

Harvey Draper
519 East State Road
American Fort, UT 84003

Frank Drew
729 Main Street
Klamath Falls, OR 97601

Duff Knives
P.O. Box 217
El Cajon, CA 92022

Gene Dumatrait
P.O. Box 3071
Beaumont, TX 77704

Leonard Dykes
15600 Pinto Way
Chino, CA 91710

Gary Ek
3180 Pembroke Road
Pembroke Park, FL 33009

Frank D. Elia
2050 Hillside Avenue
New Hyde Park, NY 11040

Virgil England
Box 10197, Klatt Station
Anchorage, AK 99502

Bob Engnath
1019 East Palmer
Glendale, CA 91205

Tom Enos
Rt. 1, Box 66
Winter Garden, FL 23787

John Evens
5414 Grissom Drive
Arlington, TX 76016

Howard Faucheaux
Box 206
Lereauville, LA 70552

Faulconer Knives
Rt. 3
Frederick, OK 73542

Thomas Ferry
4208 Canoga Drive
Woodland Hills, CA 91364

Robert Filbrun
3843 Beckwith Road
Modesto, CA 95351

L. C. Finger
1330 Nile
Corpus Christi, TX 78412

C. H. Finley
4176 St. Patrick Avenue
Redding, CA 96001

Clyde Fischer
Rt. 1, Box 170-M
Victoria, TX 77901

Mike Fisher
RFD 3
Beatrice, NB 63810

C. S. Fitch
1755 Laurel Street
Baton Rouge, LA 70802

Jim Fleming
Rt. 1, Box 784
Bonanza, OR 97683

Flint Knives
Box 9343
Olsted Falls, OH 44138

Allen Ford
3549 South Cobb Drive
Smyrna, GA 30080

William Foreman
1200 Catherine Street
Metropolis, IL 62960

Fox Knives
P.O. Box 2130, Hog Hill
Hickory, NC 28601

Edward Francek
634 North Kingsley Drive
Los Angeles, CA 90004

H. H. Frank
1 Mountain Meadow Road
Whitefish, MT 59937

Mike Franklin
Box 88
Aberdeen, OH 45101

Ron Frazier
Rt. 6, Box 212
Powhatan, VA 23139

A. J. Freiling
4082 Adams Court
Wheaton, MD 20902

W. T. Fuller
400 South Eighth Street
East Gadsden, AL 35903

Fuller-Hall Knives
P.O. Box 734
Livingston, AL 35470

Joe Funderberg
P.O. Box 582
Arcadia, CA 91006

James Furlow
4838 Santa Fe Trail
Atlanta, GA 30340

Clay Gault
P.O. Box 1347
Austin, TX 78767

Rick Genovese
2838 North Prospect Street
Colorado Springs, CO 80908

Robert Gess
Wolfe Point, MO 59201

Jim Giovanetti
2710 Denison Street
San Pedro, CA 90731

Wayne Goddard
473 Durham Avenue
Eugene, OR 79402

Ted Goldenberg
Box 3101
Walnut Creek, CA 94598

Charles Graham
P.O. Box 11
Eolia, MO 63344

Larry Grant
Box 404
Auburn, WY 83111

Rendon Griffin
9706 Cedardale
Houston, TX 77055

Walter Grigg
1303 Stetson Street
Orlando, FL 32804

Jim Grow
1712 Carlisle Road
Oklahoma City, OK 73120

Robert Hajovsky
Box 21
Scotland, TX 76379

Lloyd Hale
Rt. 2, Box 254-A
Lowell, AR 72745

Hales Knives
1742 Corning Avenue
Memphis, TN 38127

Burt Hanson
440 North 21st Street
Las Vegas, NV 89901

Jim Hardenbrook
General Delivery
Silverton, CO 81433

Harrison & Son
Box 42
Edom, TX 75756

Oscar Harwood
903 South Cooper Street
Memphis, TN 38104

Don Hastings
725 South Magnolia
Palestine, TX 75801

Tommy Having
1549 27th Street, North
Huey Town, AL 59836

Rade Hawkins
P.O. Box H
Red Oaks, GA 30272

Robert Hayes
P.O. Box 141
Railroad Flats, CA 95248

Lou Hegedus
P.O. Box 54
Forsythe, GA 31029

L. T. Hein
3515 Four Mile Road
Racine, WI 53404

Henry Heller
4107 Keeler Court
Pasadena, TX 77503

Larry Hendricks
9919 East Apache
Mesa, AZ 85207

D. E. Henry
Star Route
Mountain Ranch, CA 95246

Wayne Hensley
469 Hilltop Road
Conyers, GA 30207

George Herron
920 Murrah Avenue
Aiken, SC 29801

Ron Hewitt
Box 632
Ludowici, GA 31316

Vernon Hicks
Rt. 1, Box 387
Bauxite, AR 72011

Don Hoffman
P.O. Box 174
San Miguel, CA 93451

D'Alton Holder
6808 North 30th Drive
Phoenix, AZ 85017

Paul Holguin
2015 Lees Avenue
Long Beach, CA 90815

Jess Horn
Box 1274
Redding, CA 96001

David Howie
P.O. Box 5204
Pine Bluff, AR 71601

Fred Hoy
3303 Kerckoff Street
San Pedro, CA 90731

Arthur Hubbard
574 Cutlers Farm Road
Monroe, CT 06468

Chubby Hueske
4808 Tamerisk Drive
Bellaire, TX 77401

Jerry Hunt
4606 Princeton
Garland, TX 75040

Billy Mace Imel
1616 Bundy Avenue
New Castle, ID 47362

Dan and Ron Isaacs
3701 Eureka, Spc. 59-A
Anchorage, AK 99503

Gerry Jean
633-D Center Street
Manchester, CT 06040

Jewel Knives
609 East Twentieth Street
Tifton, GA 31794

Sid Jobs
1513 Martin Chapel Road
Murray, KY

Gordon Johnson
5426 Sweetbriar
Houston, TX 77017

LaDow Johnson
23222 West Country Club
  Parkway
Toledo, OH 43614

R. B. Johnson
Box 11
Clearwater, MN 55320

Ruffin Johnson
215 La Fonda
Houston, TX 77060

Steve Johnson
202 East Second Street,
  North
Manti, UT 84642

J. Fred Jones
858 East First Street
Ontario, CA 91762

Jolly Jones
1240 Abbot Avenue
Campbell, CA 95008

Karlin Knives
Box 668
Aztec, NM 87410

Robert Kellogg
Rt. 4, Box 181
Monroe, LA 71201

Gary Kelly
17485 Pheasant Lane
Aloha, OR 97005

Jon Kirk
800 North Olive Street
Fayetteville, AR 72701

Walter Kneubuhler
P.O. Box 327
Pioneer, OH 43554

Korvals Knives
Box 14130
Columbus, OH 44138

Dan Kvitka
17600 Superior Street
Northridge, CA 91324

Ron Lake
38 Illini Drive
Taylorville, IL 62568

Steve Landers
3817 Northwest 125th
   Street
Oklahoma City, OK 73120

Donald Lane
Rt. 4, Box 287-B
Blackfeet, ID 83221

Lane Bros.
Rt. 5
Carbondale, IL 62901

Leach Knives
5377 West Grand Blanc
   Road
Swartz Creek, MI 48073

John LeBlanc
P.O. 81
Sulphur, LA 70663

Lee Knives
Rt. 2, Box 463
Gaffney, SC 29340

Howard Lemery
Box 98
Knoxboro, NY 13362

A. R. Leppert
17718 Rhoda Street
Encino, CA 91316

Norman Levine
915 Tascosa Drive,
   Southeast
Huntsville, AL 35802

John Lienenmann
635 Grand Avenue
Billings, MT 59102

Jimmy Lile
Rt. 1
Russellville, AR 72801

Bob Lofgreen
Rt. 1, Box 395
Lakeside, AZ 85929

R. W. Loveless
Box 7836
Riverside, CA 92503

Mike Lovett
34 Taylor Street
Scottsboro, AL 35768

Robert Ludwig
1028 Pecos Avenue
Port Arthur, TX 77640

Ernie Lyle
4501 Meadow Brook
   Avenue
Orlando, FL 32808

Mac Lyle
P.O. Box 3555, CRS
Rock Hill, SC 29730

Clinton Manley
Rt. 1, Box 28
Zolfo Springs, FL 33890

Walt Mapes
2401 Estes
Lakewood, CO 80215

Larry L. Marchant
2005 North Park
Tifton, GA 31974

Joe Martin
Box 6552
Lubbock, TX 79413

Dave Marx
40 Erie Street
Tonawanda, NY 14150

R. L. Masek
Rt. 2, Box 180
David City, NB 68632

Gipsey Maxwell
219 Lenore
Jackson, TN 38301

Lindsay Maxwell
2787 Olympic, Warehouse
   Plaza 8
Springfield, OR 97477

Jerry McAlpin
Bullard, TX 77640

Harry McAvoy
2155 Tremont Boulevard,
   Northwest
Grand Rapids, MI 49504

Harvey McBurnette
Rt. 4, Box 337
Piedmont, AL 36272

Charles McConnel
158 Genteel Ridge
Wellsburg, WV 26070

Lester McFarland
Box 2732
Opelika, AL 36801

Daryl Meier
R.R. 4
Carbondale, IL 62901

Max Meyer
418 Jolee
Richardson, TX 75080

Paul Meyers
128 Twelfth Street
Wood River, IL 62095

Bill Miller
Box 434
Ashford, AL 35648

John Mims
620 South 28th
   Avenue
Hattisburg, MI 39401

Mitchell Knives
511 Avenue B
Houston, TX 77587

William F. Moran
Rt. 5
Frederick, MD 21701

Morseth Knives
1705 Highway 71, North
Springdale, AR 72764

James Moser, Jr.
17432 Market Lane
Huntington Beach, CA
   92647

Gary Mulholland
Box 93
Davenport, CA 95017

Pete Mumford
Box 3
Farisita, CO 81037

Woody Naifeh
Rt. 13, Box 380
Tulsa, OK 74107

Ivan Nealey
c/o Rocky Bar Stage
Mountain Home, ID 83647

Jim Nolen
P.O. Box 6217
Corpus Christi, TX 78411

R. D. Nolen
Box 2895
Estes Park, CO 80517

Robert Ogg
Rt. 1, Box 230
Paris, AR 72855

Robert Oleson
800 Keokuk Street
Petaluma, CA 94952

W. C. Overholster
235 Northeast Eleventh
  Street
Newport, OR 97365

John Owens, Jr.
8755 Southwest 96th Street
Miami, FL 33156

Howard Palmer
2031 Tronjo Road
Pensacola, FL 32503

Philip Pankiewicz
RFD 1, Waterman Road
Lebanon, CT 06249

Melvin Pardue
P.O. Box 14357
Tampa, FL 33690

F. D. Parrish
2528 East McKellips
Mesa, AZ 85203

W. C. Pass
1455 Phyllis Drive
Merritt Island, FL 32952

W. D. Pease
Rt. 1, Box 305
Ripley, OH 45167

Pepper Knives
2102 Spencer
Monroe, LA 71201

Pharris Knives
6247 Whitecliff Way
North Highlands, CA
  95660

David Pitt
36601 Leone Street
Newark, CA 94560

Leon Pittman
Rt. 1
Pendergrass, GA 30567

Dick Planas
516 Double Street
Carson, CA 90745

Paul Poehlmann
Box 445
Stinson Beach, CA 94970

Jerry Poletis
Box 1582
Scottsdale, AZ 85252

Jim Poplin
401 Pineview Drive
Mt. Airy, NC 27030

Ed Pou
322 Cleveland Street
New Albany, MI 38652

Wesley Powell
7211 Tropicana Street
Miramar, FL 33023

Jerry Price
P.O. Box 782
Springdale, AR 72764

Ralph Prouty
5240 Southwest 49th Street
Portland, OR 97405

Jim Pugh
917 Carpenter Street
Azle, TX 76020

Bill Pugsley
1255½ West Twelfth Street
Eugene, OR 97402

Melvin Purdue
P.O. Box 14357
Tampa, FL 33690

Aaron Pursley
Bear Paw Route 6-A
Big Sandy, MT 59520

Don Puterbaugh
Knife Gallery
4062 Templeton
Colorado Springs, CO 80907

Ray Quincy
Box 1851
Paso Robles, CA 93446

Randall Made Knives
Box 1988
Orlando, FL 38202

R. J. Read, Jr.
916 Neartop Drive
Nashville, TN 37205

Jim Richards
170 23rd Street
Costa Mesa, CA 92627

Charles Richardson
Box 38329
Dallas, TX 75238

Gay Rocha
General Delivery
Glide, OR 97443

Joe Rodriquez
5241 Josephine Street
Lynwood, CA 90262

Richard Romano
31 Arlington Road
Windsor Locks, CT 06096

John Roy
P.O. Box 191
Veneta, OR 97487

R. H. Ruana
Box 527
Bonner, MT 59823

Russ Blades
P.O. Box 7214
Spokane, WA 99207

Jody Samson
Box 1423
Burbank, CA 91507

Jim Sasser
1811 Santa Fe Drive
Pueblo, CO 81006

J. Schmidt
R.D.R. Eastern Avenue
Ballston Lake, NY 12019

Ray Schmidt
Track Knives
1313 Second Street
Whitefish, MT 59937

Jack Schmier
16767 Mulberry Circle
Fountain Valley, CA 92708

Clifton Schneck
P.O. Box 1017
Bonners Ferry, ID 83805

H. J. Schneider
24296 Via Aquara
Laguna Niguel, CA 92677

Maurice Schrock & Son
1708 South Plum Street
Pontiac, MI 61764

John Schwarz
41 Fifteenth Street
Wellsburg, WV 26070

Jim Serven
6153 Third Street
Mayville, MI

David Shaw
2009 North 450
East Ogden, UT 84404

Sheldon Knives
P.O. Box 1343
Frederick, MD 21701

Ben Shelor
Rt. 14, Box 318-B
Richmond, VA 23231

Dave Shirley
39723 Plumas Way
Fremont, CA 94538

Corbet Sigman
Rt. 1, Box 212-A
Liberty, WV 26070

Silver Fox Knives
2001 Lenze
LaMarque, TX 77568

Bert Simmons
1776 South Jackson
Suite 407
Denver, CO 80210

Jim Small, Jr.
474 Foster Street
Madison, GA 30650

Cary Smith
804 Carnation Avenue
Metairie, LA 70001

Fred R. Smith
8072 Dorian Way
Fair Oaks, CA 95628

Jim Smith
1608 JoAnn
Wichita, KA 67203

John T. Smith
8404 Cedar Crest Drive
Southaven, MI 38671

W. J. Sonneville
1050 Chalet Drive West
Mobile, AL 36608

Bernard Sparks
Box 32
Dingle, ID 83233

C. R. Staudinger
37 Beverly Place
Utica, NY 13501

George Stone
259 Arapahoe Central Park
Richardson, TX 75080

D. L. Stranahan
Box 2812
Oxnard, CA 93030

Gray Taylor
137 Lana View Drive
Kingsport, TN 37664

Terrill Custom Knives
P.O. Box 669
Lindsay, CA 93247

Leroy Thayer
15600 Pinto Way
Chino, CA 91710

Bill Thomason
167 Lower Dawnville Road,
  Northeast
Dalton, GA 30720

Danny Thornton
P.O. Box 334
Fort Mill, SC 29715

Bob Tice
219 Park Avenue
Franklin, OH 45005

Ron Tice
5938 U.S. 22
New Holland, OH 73120

Carolyn D. Tinker
1699 North Marengo Avenue
Pasadena, CA 91103

P. J. Tomes
100 Lundie Lane
Petersburg, VA 23803

R. J. Tomes
41 Greenbrier
Hampton, VA 23661

Dwight Towell
Rt. 1
Midvale, ID 83645

Virgil Dee Tye
901 South Chester Avenue
Bakersfield, CA 95017

Vairag Knives
111 Marine Street
Davenport, CA 75017

Edie Vaughn
1905 Virginia Drive
Grand Prairie, TX 75050

Howard Viele
88 Lexington Avenue
Westwood, NJ 07675

Frank Vought, Jr.
P.O. Box 62
Plattenville, LA 70393

Buster Warenski
P.O. Box 214
Richfield, UT 84701

Weatherford Bros.
4775 Memphis Drive
Dallas, TX 75207

F. E. Weber
401 West Clinton Street
Haledon, NJ 07508

D. E. Weiler
Box 1576
Yuma, AZ 85364

Charles Weiss
18847 North Thirteenth
  Avenue
Phoenix, AZ 85027

Mike Wesolowski
902-A Lohrman Lane
Petaluma, CA 94952

Bob Whitaker
4633 Derta Road
Memphis, TN 38109

W.H.W. Knives
P.O. Box 7017
Fort Wayne, IN 46807

Horace Wiggins
Box 152
Mansfield, LA 71052

W. C. Wilber
400 Lucerne Drive
Spartanburg, SC 29302

W. C. Williams
Rt. 2, Box 452
Atlanta, TX 75551

R. W. Wilson
P.O. Box 2012
Weirton, WV 26062

Art Wiman
P.O. Box 92
Plummerville, AR 72127

Bill Winn
Star Route
Grover, TX 79040

Wood Knives
38 South Venice Boulevard
Venice, CA 90291

Richard Worthen
834 Carnation Drive
Sandy, UT 84070

Bob Wrench
P.O. Box 10914
Eugene, OR 80517

Tim Wright
5831 South Blackstone
Chicago, IL 60637

Gary Wyman
6047 Pitcairn Street
Cypress, CA 90630

T. J. Yancy
P.O. Box 943
Estes Park, CO 80517

David York
213 Ben Lomand Drive
McMinnville, TN 37110

Don Zaccagnino
Box ZACK
Pahokee, FL 33476

William Zalewski
97 Evans Avenue
East Hartford, CT 06118

Richard Zeller
1209 Davis
Fairborn, OH 45324

ENGRAVERS

Winston Churchill
Twenty Mile Stream Road
Proctorsville, VT 05153

J. R. French
855 Substation Road
Brunswick, OH 44212

Lance Kelly
4226 Lamar Street
Decatur, GA 30035

Lynton McKenzie
R. J. Hodgson & Sons
5598 Arapahoe, Unit 104
Boulder, CO 80301

Ray Mellen
Box 101
Winston, GA 30187

A. Pietett
Hawk Hollow Road
Denver, NY 12421

Joe Rundell
6198 Frances Road
Clio, MI 48420

George Sherwood
1128 Page Road
Sherwood, OR 97495

Ron Skaggs
508 West Central
Princeton, IL 61356

Robert Valade
Rt. 1, Box 30-A
Cove, OR 97824

ETCHERS

Shaw–Leibowitz
Rt. 1, Box 421
New Cumberland, WV 26047

SCRIMSHANDERS

O. M. Barringer
P.O. Box 1232
Port Richey, FL 33568

Michael Collins
Rt. 4
Batesville Road
Woodstock, GA 30188

W. C. Frazier
1029 Kavanaugh Street
Mansfield, LA 71052

Don Haynes
P.O. Box 131
Murrells Inlet, SC 29576

Gene Hooper
Gentryville, IN 47537

Wm. Metcalf
P.O. Box 861
Portersville, CA 93257

Joe Rundall
6198 Frances Road
Clio, MI 48420

R. E. Skaggs
508 West Central
Princeton, MI 49875

Glen Sterns
224½ Huron Street
Toledo, OH 43605

Ann Yancy
P.O. Box 943
Estes Park, CO 80417

SHEATH MAKERS

Craig Floyd
Box 145
Bunker Hill, IN 46914

Jesse W. Smith Saddlery
East 3024 Sprague
Spokane, WA 99201

Walt Whinnery
1947 Meadow Creek Drive
Louisville, KY 40281

MACHINES AND HEAVY EQUIPMENT

Bader Grinder Co.
Valley Falls, NY 12185

Filmore & Gaber, Inc.
1742 Floradale Avenue
South El Monte, CA 91733

Jim Kier
P.O. Box 13522
Arlington, TX 76013

Olympic Equipment Co.
Box 80187
Seattle, WA 98108

Speed Cut Belt Grinder Co.
P.O. Box 399
333 College Avenue
Ephriam, UT 84627

CUTLERY SUPPLIERS

Anderson Knives
R.D. 4, Shepard Hill Road
Newton, CT 06470

Angus-Campbell, Inc.
4417 South Soto Street
Los Angeles, CA 90058

Atlanta Cutlery Co.
Box 839
Conyers, GA 30207

Brownells, Inc.
Rt. 2, Box 1
Montezuma, IA 50171

Bykem Co.
8501 Delpert Drive
St. Louis, MO 63114

Crazy Crow Trading Co.
1301 Cole Drive
Denison, TX 75020

Custom Knifemakers's
Supply
P.O. Box 308
Emory, TX 75440

Golden Age Arms Co.
14 West Winter Street
Box 283
Delaware, OH 43015

House of Muzzleloading
P.O. Box 6217-A
Glendale, CA 91205

Knife & Gun Finishing
Supplies
2112 Meadow Lake Court
Arlington, TX 76013

Knife World
4361 South Broadway
Englewood, CO 80110

R & W Cutlery Supplies
P.O. Box 630
San Rafael, CA 94901

Sheffield Knifemakers
Supply
P.O. Box 3011
St. Augustine, FL 32084

Van Sickle Cutlery
P.O. Box 3081
San Antonio, TX 76901

HEAT-TREATING SHOPS

Barbee Knives
Box 1702
Fort Stockton, TX 79735

Benedick-Miller
Orient Way
Lyndhurst, NJ 07071

Hauni-Richmond, Inc.
5100 Charles City Road
Richmond, VA 23231

Pacific Heat Treating Co.
1238 Birchwood Drive
Sunnyvale, CA 94086

Paul Bos
2320 Yucca Hill Drive
Alpine, CA 92001

Proto Shop
3020 North Stone Street
Colorado Springs, CO 80907

SHARPENING EQUIPMENT

From most suppliers listed
and from:

Loray Sharpeners
R.D. 2
Grafton, OH 44044

A. G. Russell Co.
1705 Highway 71 North
Springdale, AR 72764

Custom Purveyors
P.O. Box 886
Fort Lee, NJ 07024

Ramrod Gun & Knife Shop
State Road 3 North
New Castle, IN 47362

Gillie & Co.
205 East Putnam Avenue
Cos Cob, CT 06807

A. G. Russell Co.
1705 Highway 71 North
Springdale, AR 72764

KNIFE SHOPS AND DEALERS

Acorn Shop
Gatlinburg, TN 37738

Hales Knives
1795 Dellwood
Memphis, TN 38127

The Knife Shop
El Paso International Airport
El Paso, TX 79925

Bill's Custom Knives
R.D. 1, Box 163
Waymart, PA 18472

Knife World
4361 South Broadway
Englewood, CO 80110

The Knife Store
1795 Dellwood
Memphis, TN 38127

Technical Notes:

Many knifemakers have asked what equipment I have used in taking photographs of knives and knifemaking. The cameras are Olympus OM-1 models with automatic winders. Lenses most used are a 50-mm Macro F3.5 and a 35-mm F2. Lamps are two Smith Victor quartz iodine lamps in miniature reflectors bounced off silver Reflectasol umbrellas. Film is FP 4 and HP 5, manufactured by Ilford in England.

INDEX

Numbers in italic type refer to illustrations.